If you live he

and vote on t

Alabama: none. **Alaska*:** all home rule cities including Anchorage, Fairbanks, Juneau. **Arizona*:** all cities and counties, ranging from Aguila, Ajo, Alpine... to Winston County, Woodville, York. **Arkansas*:** all cities and counties, ranging from Alma, Altheimer, Ahus... to Wynne, Yell County, Yellville. **California*:** all charter cities, ranging from Adelanto, Alameda, Albany... to Vernon, Visalia, Whittier. **Colorado*:** all municipalities, ranging from Arvada, Aspen, Aurora... to Westminster, Wheat Ridge, Widefield. **Connecticut:** selected towns, ranging from Berlin, Bethel, Brookfield... to Wallingford, Westhaven, Wolcott. **Delaware:** none. **District of Columbia*:** Washington. **Florida*:** all municipalities, and the home rule counties of Broward, Dade, Jacksonville, Pinellas, Sarasota, Volusia. **Georgia:** all municipalities. **Hawaii:** just the island counties, Hawaii, Honolulu, Kauai, Maui. **Idaho*:** all cities and counties, ranging from Aberdeen, Ada County, Adams County... to Weston, Wilder, Winchester. **Iowa:** only Iowa City. **Illinois*:** all municipalities, ranging from Abingdon, Addison, Albany... to Yorkville, Zeigler, Zion. **Indiana:** none. **Kansas:** all municipalities, ranging from Abilene, Alma, Almena... to Winchester, Winfield, Yates Center. **Kentucky:** City and County of Lexington, only. **Louisiana:** 16 parishes, ranging from Ascension, Caddo, East Baton Rouge... to St. Mary, Tangipahoa, Terrebonne. **Maine*:** all charter jurisdictions, all major cities, ranging from Aroostock, Augusta, Bangor... to Westbrook, Winslow, Yarmouth. **Maryland:** all counties and chartered cities, ranging from Allegany, Anne Arundel, Baltimore City... to Westminster, Wicomico, Worcester. **Massachusetts*:** most major cities, ranging from Abington, Adams, Amesbury... to Winthrop, Woburn, Worcester. **Michigan*:** all chartered cities, ranging from Adrian, Albion, Algonac... to Yipsilanti, Zeeland, Zilwaukee. **Minnesota:** charter cities, ranging from Ada, Albert Lea, Alexandria... to Winona, Winthrop, Worthington. **Mississippi*:** none. **Missouri*:** all chartered cities and counties. **Montana*:** all cities and counties. **Nebraska*:** all cities and towns. **Nevada*:** all cities and counties, ranging from Alamo, Austin, Battle Mountain... to Wolfsboro, Wolfsboro Falls, Woodville. **New Hampshire:** 21 chartered cities and towns, ranging from Bedford, Berlin, Concord... to Rochester, Seabrook, Somersworth. **New Jersey:** all commission and council cities, ranging from Asbury Park, Atlantic City, Audubon... to Moorestown, Morristown, Wyckoff. **New Mexico:** all counties, all cities with commission-manager governments, ranging from Aztec, Carlsbad, Gallup... to Raton, Tucumcari, Truth or Consequences. **New York:** all chartered cities, ranging from Albany, Amsterdam, Arlington... to White Plains, Woodmere, Yonkers. **North Carolina:** all chartered cities, ranging from Albemarle, Asheboro, Asheville... to Wrightsville Beach, Woodfin, Yadkinville. **North Dakota*:** all commission and home rule cities, ranging from Bismark, Dickinson, Grand Forks... to Wahpeton, West Fargo, Williston. **Ohio*:** all 196 municipalities, ranging from Akron, Amberly, Ashland... to Wyoming, Xenia, Yellow Springs. **Oklahoma*:** all municipalities, ranging from Ada, Altus,

Ardmore... to Warr Acres, Weatherford, Yukon. **Oregon*:** chartered cities, ranging from Albany, Astoria, Beaverton... to St. Helena, The Dalles, Tualatin. **Pennsylvania:** 48 cities with commissioner governments, home rule counties and municipalities, ranging from Bethel Park, Carbondale City, Chalfont Borough... to Whitehall Township, Whitemarsh Township, Wilkes-Barre Township. **Rhode Island:** only East Providence, Newport, North Kingston. **South Carolina:** all cities and counties, ranging from Abbeville, Abbeville County, Aiken... to Yemassee, York, York County. **South Dakota*:** all cities and counties, ranging from Aberdeen, Alcester, Alexandria... to Yankton, Yankton County, Ziebach County. **Tennessee:** selected charter cities and counties, including Chattanooga, Knox County, Knoxville, Nashville, Shelby County. **Texas:** 217 home rule cities, ranging from Abilene, Addison, Alamo... to Woodville, Wylie, Yoakum. **Utah*:** all cities and counties, ranging from Alta, American Fork, Aurora... to West Valley City, Willard, Woods Cross. **Vermont:** all municipalities, ranging from Alburg, Arlington, Bakersfield... to Winoski, Winoski Park, Woodstock. **Virginia:** only Hampton, Norfolk, Portsmouth, Richmond. **Washington*:** all major cities and five counties — Clallam, King, Pierce, Snohomish, Whatcom. **West Virginia:** all chartered cities, ranging from Addison, Albright, Alderson... to Winfield, Womelsdorff, Worthington. **Wisconsin:** all cities, ranging from Abbotsford City, Adams City, Adel... to Wyeville Village, Wyoeena Village, Yuba Village. **Wyoming:*** none. **Note:** This is an unofficial list. See inside back cover.

Listed above are the local jurisdictions where initiatives to establish term limits seem possible, based on a national review of local laws. Also, * indicates every state where statewide initiatives are possible for this purpose. (Illinois is a special case, since it permits petitioning only for limits on state officials, pending litigation now in process.)

Since sample jurisdictions are listed alphabetically, this indicates nothing about the need for term limits or the desire of local residents to establish them. For instance, Yuba Village, Wisconsin, cast 40 votes in the last gubernatorial election. Six signatures will place on its ballot the issue of limiting terms of its city officials. However, in a village this size, it is a moral certainty everyone in town knows what the government is doing and speaks up personally if changes are needed. Not every jurisdiction where limits are possible, has any apparent need for them.

At the opposite end of the scale is Virginia. Only four of its jurisdictions permit petitioning on limits. It is a moral certainty that some places in Virginia badly need term limits, but citizens cannot petition and vote on them. The most restrictive states are Alabama, Delaware, Indiana, Mississippi and Wyoming which apparently have no initiative process for any purpose, at the local level.

Regarding all jurisdictions, this summary was prepared by laymen and lawyers working at a distance. Advice from local counsel should always be sought about the applicable features of local law on petition drives for term limits, or any other subject.

Why Term Limits?

Because They Have It Coming!

John Charles Armor

JAMESON BOOKS, INC.
OTTAWA, ILLINOIS

Published by
Jameson Books, Inc.
722 Columbus Street
Ottawa, Illinois 61350

Jameson Books are available at special discounts for bulk purchases for sales promotions, premiums, fundraising, or educational use. Special editions, condensed editions, or book excerpts can also be created to specification. For details contact: Special Sales Director, Jameson Books, Inc., P.O. Box 738, Ottawa, Illinois 61350 or call 815-434-7905.

Distributed to the book trade by
Login Brothers Consortium
1436 West Randolph Street
Chicago, Illinois 60607
312-733-8228

First Edition

1 3 5 6 4 2

ISBN: 0915463-70-9

to

the hundreds of thousands
of ordinary Americans
who care about this nation
and who are giving freely and greatly
of their time and money
to straighten out the Congress
by establishing term limits

Contents

Graphs and Special Sections

Tables

Foreword

The first state–mandated federal term limit law, passed by the citizens of Colorado in 1990, is to the democratic system what the first volleys fired at Concord and Lexington were to the British Empire in 1775. Both represent the beginning of change and the assertion of the sovereignty of the people.

Life in politics has become a perpetual run for reelection, an exercise in self–service rather than political service.

The overwhelming urge to maintain power motivates the current system. But the term limits movement offers hope to all who believe in citizen government and the ideal of public service.

Seldom in American history have the people taken the lead as they have in the current battle for term limits. The direct election of U.S. Senators and the Women's Suffrage movement are comparable popular reforms that began with the people at the state level. Yet term limits promise to restructure our political system like no other reform since the ratification of the Constitution.

In the summer of 1994, we agreed to Co–Chair the U. S. Term Limits Council. We as Governors — one a Democrat and the other a Republican — support limits on our positions. Kansas Governors are limited to only two consecutive terms under its constitution. Massachusetts Governors will also be limited with the passage of term limits this year. We believe those limits are healthy for our states. We believe the two–term limit on the Presidency is healthy for the nation. We believe similar limits on the U.S. House and Senate will likewise be healthy for the nation. And we believe that if the people take the lead on this issue, the leaders will inevitably follow.

John Armor's book, *Why Term Limits?* is an important weapon in that battle. Armor clearly shows, with wit and wisdom, that the term limits movement is not simply a knee–jerk reaction based on popular frustration with government, but is a reasonable prescription for what ails our democracy. Term limits history, research, arguments and talking points are laid out to arm the reader against an elite political culture that is hostile to the restoration of citizen government.

This book should be considered a manual for term limits activists all across the country. It is essential reading for all who doubt the wisdom of the people.

Governor Joan Finney
(D) Kansas

Governor William F. Weld
(R) Massachusetts

Introduction

Much of what has been published and broadcast about term limits is just personal opinions, unfettered by facts. Some of it is flat–out dishonest in the interest of political self–preservation, like the comments of the Speaker of the House, Thomas Foley. But even so–called experts and supposedly impartial gurus in the Washington press corps fall into the trap of repeating false assumptions on this subject as if they were true.

The assertions in this book are backed up by real–world facts and by long–term research, much of it newly published here. To those with open minds, facts matter in concluding whether term limits for Congress, state officials, and local officials are good or bad. To those merely trying to protect their own political necks, facts are both irrelevant and unwelcome.

The need for term limits is best demonstrated by showing how congressional elections have become controlled, predictable and largely meaningless ceremonies rather than genuine reflections of public choices. This book predicts the House races in November 1994 using data as of June 13. These predictions ignore politics, personalities, support of or opposition to President Clinton, votes for or against NAFTA, the Clinton budget, or any other subject. They rely solely on incumbency and money raised. From experience in 1992, the predictions should be more than 96.7 percent accurate. If so, then Speaker Foley and other opponents of limits are wrong on the facts, and this book and the supporters of limits are right.

This book describes some of the ordinary Americans who have performed extraordinary tasks in conducting term limit campaigns against well–funded, veteran opponents, beginning with the two campaigns by citizen Sherry Bockwinkel against Speaker of the House Tom Foley.

It describes the changes over time in increased tenure of members of the House, and the doubling of the tenure of the leaders of the House, who control most of its legislative decisions, both to pass laws and to refuse to pass laws. It gives the turnover rates for the House, and the reasons for the turnover. The changes have been extraordinary, especially comparing the first 125 years with the latest 77 years.

With congressmen becoming members for life, rather than members for a few years, they have gotten far out of touch with their constituents. As a result, the public opinion of Congress has dropped, like a brick in a well, to an all–time low. Some of this is driven by specific scandals, of which there is an ample supply. But some of it is endemic; the people no longer trust or like Congress as an institution.

The result has been a steady growth in public support for term limits, to the point that a majority of all demographic groups and political groups support limits. Also, the public support has crystallized around two terms (12 years) for senators, and three terms (six years) for representatives.

The Framers of the Constitution wrote extensively on the need for "rotation in office," meaning that congressmen would serve for a limited period of time, then go home to live among their fellow citizens under the laws that they had written. As the record demonstrates, this happened voluntarily among both congressmen and presidents for most of our history.

When the voluntary restraints were broken for president, they were made mandatory by law. Now that the restraints have also been broken for Congress, it is time to make them mandatory as well.

Congress constitutes only 435 of the approximately 500,000 elected officials at the local, state and federal levels in the United States. The problem of long–term incumbents who are out of touch is less acute at the state and local levels. Still, where the people perceive this problem at those levels, they are applying the same remedy — term limits. So, an outline of the state and local limit efforts is also included.

Although each opportunity to establish limits has been created by local efforts by local citizens, all the efforts have a combined, national effect. This book describes all state and major local successes to date, those that can be, and may be, on the ballot in 1994 and 1995, and the combined effect of all of these on the ultimate, national decision on limits for all congressmen.

The debate between opponents and supporters of term limits is often described in these terms: a loss of "experience, clout, or institutional memory" by opponents, or an end to "non-responsive government" or a "restoring of citizen control" by supporters. Arguments for and against are examined in the words of the leaders of both sides, followed by a Question & Answer section on the most common challenges to limits.

Tens of thousands of Americans will be involved in 1994 as leaders in term limit campaigns. Millions more will vote for or against limits, this year and next. The strategy and tactics of both supporters and opponents commonly used in prior campaigns and to be expected in campaigns to come, are described.

The US Supreme Court has just agreed to hear a test case from Arkansas on the constitutionality of term limits. This case will probably determine the legal fate of the hundreds of state and local term limit initiatives in the last four years, and under way now. The outcome of that case is analyzed and predicted in plain English, rather than lawyerese.

The final question is how congressional term limits can go from sometimes different state–based initiatives in 23 states, to a single, national standard. This book describes how garden variety politics in Congress will change die–hard opposition into willingness to pass a national limit on terms for Congress.

Finally, the book includes a Technical Appendix of statistical tables, references to legal cases and sources, and historical data to support the conclusions stated. And it includes a bibliography — selected reference to major sources of information on term limits, so researchers, reporters, teachers and others with an insatiable desire for information on limits can find all they want.

The author of this book makes no bones about his support for term limits. However, every number and every fact used to support limits or to question the positions of those who oppose limits, can be checked and verified by anyone, including opponents. Perhaps the best starting point is the apparent paradox that voters approve term limits at the same time they reelect their incumbent congressmen. This is only a paradox if both elections offer free and fair choices. If one election is fair and the other is a stacked deck, then the difference makes sense.

Prompted by Speaker Tom Foley and his ilk, the press tends to report simultaneous victories for term limits initiatives and for incumbents in the same election as a paradox. The conclusion drawn is that voters really don't mean one or the other. Usually, the pundits assert that the voters don't mean term limits, that in these votes the people are just "acting out" like fractious two–year–olds.

These two types of elections are in a sense similar. In both, the incumbents are running against a challenger. But it is like running a 100–yard race twice between the same competitors, only the second time the "incumbent" runner gets a 50–yard head start. In the fair race, the challenger wins big. In the fixed race, the incumbent wins big. There is no contradiction. Properly understood, both results make sense at the same time.

This book concludes that congressional elections are governed by the Spinach Factor. For chapter and verse about how and why this occurs, read on.

The intent of this book is to analyze a serious subject. However, humor is used as a weapon for reasons Mark Twain best explained in *The Mysterious Stranger,* in 1909:

> Power, money, persuasion, supplication, persecution — these can lift at a colossal humbug — push it a little — weaken it a little, century by century; but only laughter can blow it to atoms at a single blast. Against the assault of laughter nothing can stand.

This writer believes the present conduct of Congress is a colossal humbug, as is the sanctimonious defense of it by Speaker Foley. So, Mark Twain's advice has been followed.

The author has talked with more than two hundred people involved in the term limits effort, from citizens who vote on the issue, to supporters who work in campaigns, to current officeholders at the local, state and federal levels who support term limits. All agree on two points. One is that term limits are a necessary change in American government today. The other is that term limits are *not* a partisan issue between the Democratic and Republican Parties.

> ***The Spinach Factor***
>
> Reelection of incumbents is to voters as spinach to small children. How much we get is a false measure of how much we want. But unlike spinach, incumbents aren't "good for you."

As the record clearly demonstrates, and this book documents in eight of its eleven chapters, the contest on term limits is between long–term office holders of *both* political parties, and short–term officeholders and members of *both* political parties, with the latter better representing the views of the people. Recent elections held in 15 states and three of the nation's four largest cities show that term limits are succeeding only because they have bipartisan support. No initiative can possibly pass in New York City without majority support from Democratic voters; term limits had that, solidly.

Some opponents of term limits portray them as an issue of Democrats vs. Republicans. Some political scientists have done the same. And some "experts" in the press have advanced the same argument. But on the facts — and the facts are laid out in this book — that argument is false. It is a red herring intended to distract voters from following what they know is the better choice for this nation.

As Governors Finney and Weld note in the Foreword, term limits are one of those few issues on which the people are the leaders, and elected leaders will be compelled to follow. The leaders for limits are members of both major political parties, plus independents and members of other political parties. No issue that has the demonstrated support of two–thirds of the American people can be honestly described as an effort by *either* the Democratic or Republican Parties. Term limits are bigger and broader than that.

Many people have been helpful in the writing of this book. Two in particular should be mentioned by name. Julie Riggs, Director of Term Limits Everywhere! has minded details in hundreds of jurisdictions at once. Norm Leahy, Research Director of US Term Limits, has been invaluable. Without the efforts of these two people, this book could not have been written.

1

David and Goliath

A key scene in the movie *Network* occurred when the news anchor (Peter Finch) went berserk on live TV. He ran to the camera and demanded that listeners go to their windows, throw them open, and shout, "I'm mad as hell, and I'm not going to take it any more." Cut to a rain-drenched street bordered by tall apartment buildings. A few people appear and shout, then dozens, then thousands take up the cry, "I'm mad as hell, and I'm not going to take it any more." This kind of deep-seated anger is behind the drive for term limits today.

Sherry Bockwinkel is a businesswoman, environmental writer and activist in Tacoma. She is also a Democrat. She has never held public office. But she was mad as hell in 1991 about the hammerlock held by incumbents in Washington State. So she went straight to the top. She attacked Thomas Foley, Congressman from Washington, Speaker of the House of Representatives, and the second most powerful man in the federal government.

She fought him head to head on an issue of life or death importance to Speaker Foley. In November 1991 she lost.

She wasn't running for his seat in Congress. She was campaigning to bar all members in the House or Senate who had served as long as Foley. Her issue was term limits for Congress. Undaunted by initial defeat, she demanded a rematch.

In November 1992 this businesswoman and civic leader defeated Speaker Foley. He had the support of Philip Morris, RJR Nabisco, Northrup, General Electric, many labor organizations, and the National Rifle Association. All she had was the support of 1,119,985 voters in Washington State. The term limits initiative passed, providing that no senator could serve more than two consecutive terms (12 years), and no congressman could serve more than three consecutive terms (six years).

After being rebuked by the voters of his state on this critical issue, Speaker Foley and several fronts for his position, including, sadly, the League of Women Voters, attacked the verdict of the people in court. Foley sued the state of Washington — in effect, sued his own citizens — asking the court to throw out their judgment and substitute Foley's judgment that he should continue to serve as long as he can draw breath.

A federal trial court sided with the Foley Forces and overturned the judgment of the people of Washington. That case is, as this is written, on appeal in the Court of Appeals for the Ninth Circuit. In time, it may become part of the test case in the US Supreme Court. On June 20, 1994, the Court accepted for review *US Term Limits v. Thornton,* the split decision of the Arkansas Supreme Court upholding term limits for state officials, but striking them down for federal officials. But that is a story for another chapter.

The subject here is the kind of people who are stepping forward, state by state and city by city, to lead the petition efforts. Why are the people responding so readily to the term limit petitions, first in signing to get limits on the ballot, then in voting by an average margin of 67 percent to 33 percent to establish limits by law?

What fired up Sherry Bockwinkel and the people in Washington State so that they took on the most powerful politician in their state and beat him? Why were the people of 14 other states mad enough to pass their own term limits for members of Congress, one in 1990 and the others in 1992 along with Washington? And, why are the people of seven more states about to do the same thing in the election of 1994?

As this is written, the status in 1994 seems likely to be seven new states acting on term limits for Congress. Nebraska will repeat what it did in 1992 to send a message to politicians and to its Supreme Court. Colorado will vote again, to lower the limits on its representatives to three terms, rather than the six-term limit in its 1990 initiative. Illinois *may* vote on term limits for state officials only. And the District of Columbia will vote on limits for District officials only.

Some of these are certain as this is written, others depend on petition efforts or litigation still under way. In July, the Oklahoma Supreme Court denied an effort by term limit opponents to knock the issue off its ballot. Governor David Walters strongly endorsed term limits, in setting the issue for vote on September 20, the date of the state's primary run-off elections. September will be the first bellwether for term limits in 1994.

Also in July, a trial judge in Illinois knocked term limits off the ballot because the convention that wrote that state's constitution did not discuss term limits when creating the initiative process. Since the purpose of Illinois initiatives is

> ***The Tyrannosaurus Conclusion***
>
> With two-ton bodies and two-ounce brains, the tyrannosaurs were dimly aware that they were alive. On term limits, the same applies to the leaders of Congress. They are politically extinct, but haven't gotten the word.

to deal with issues the legislature does not, or will not, address, this decision is ludicrous. Supporters of limits have asked the Illinois Supreme Court to reverse the trial judge and put limits back on the ballot.

The plaintiff in Illinois was the Chicago Bar Association, one more indication of the marriage of lawyers to the status quo on the subject of limits. The American Trial Lawyers Association and its affiliates are also frequent contributors to opponents of term limits.

In Arkansas, the term limits movement was already under way when a critical member was drawn into it by circumstance. Tim Jacob, a businessman in a small family firm, was Chairman of Arkansans for Governmental Reform, Inc., with the petition for limits on state and federal officials already written, when Skip Cook signed up as a member of the Speaker's Bureau. The other two principals were Steve Munn, a computer programmer, and Tim Epperson, an engineer. All of them were political novices, with no prior experience in such a campaign.

On the other side was the Democratic Party of Arkansas, and many of its traditional associates. The leader was George Jernigan, former chairman of the state Democratic Party, lawyer, lobbyist, and sometime water boy for Governor Bill Clinton.

It looked like a mismatch. Jernigan named his organization Arkansans for Representative Democracy. It sounded good, but it didn't match the political facts of Arkansas politics, a state dominated by the Democratic Party, in turn dominated by its long-time officeholders in the legislature and in the state house. It was said of Jernigan's organization that "you couldn't find a human being in it anywhere," it being composed of corporations doing business with the state, lobbyists, and lawyers.

Skip Cook, the new man in the Speaker's Bureau, was a long-time investment banker with PaineWebber. He signed up because he agreed with the issue, and he knew how to speak, being past president of a Little Rock Toastmasters Club. He got heavily involved.

In February 1992 it became clear the supporters of term limits would be overwhelmed by their opposition without serious fundraising. With the encouragement of his family, Skip Cook resigned as a broker, took a huge reduction in salary, and became a fundraiser for "Term Limits Now," which the organization used as its simpler, public name.

In time, 'Term Limits Now" exceeded the $140,000 its opponents raised by $20,000. In April 1992 Cook also took over the flagging petition drive. On July 3, they turned in 90,000 signatures, well over the 69,641 required.

Immediately, the opponents filed suit, trying to knock the issue off the ballot. The case reached the Supreme Court of Arkansas which allowed the issue to go on the ballot, but reserved judgment on its constitutionality. On election day in November 1992 term limits got a higher proportion of yes votes of votes cast, than native son Bill Clinton got of the presidential vote in Arkansas.

The people had spoken. For good measure, they defeated George Jernigan in his later bid to become lieutenant governor, to fill the slot left open after Governor Clinton became president and his lieutenant governor moved up.

But, the battle was not over. As Jernigan said, the day after the term limit victory, "I don't know who I'll find to file suit, but I'll find somebody." The litigation continued, with the League of Women Voters among the cat's paws for the Democratic Party in the case.

The League's position was surprising, given the fossilization of Arkansas politics. In 1992, of the 135 members of the Arkansas legislature, 86 faced *no opposition whatsoever,* neither primary nor general election opponents. In 1994, the no-contest incumbents dropped to 54.

Then, in March 1994 the Arkansas Supreme Court ruled, as had the California Supreme Court before it, that term limits for state officials were entirely constitutional. The California case had been taken to the US Supreme Court, which refused to hear the case. So, statewide term limits were a *fait accompli* in Arkansas.

Although the Arkansas limits will not start excluding state officials from the ballot until 1998, the effects are already being felt. About a dozen long-term legislators resigned from safe seats, some to become lobbyists, some to return to law practice, some to run for other offices. After the recommendation of a "nonpartisan" commission, the legislature decided to use free voting in the party caucuses to choose leaders in the house and senate, rather than the long-established seniority system. The first fruits of term limits were a breath of change in Arkansas politics.

The final chapter in the term limit story there is yet to be written. The part of the Arkansas case that struck down term limits for congressional members only, was accepted for review by the US Supreme Court, with the decision expected sometime early in 1995.

As for Skip Cook, he ran for the legislature as a Democrat and "was beaten, fair and square." He has found a new career as a construction executive and is rebuilding his private life. But he has no doubts about the massive commitment he and his family made in order to make term limits a reality in Arkansas. He says, "If I had it to do over again, I'd do it all the same way."

Among the other ordinary people who did extraordinary things in term limits efforts across the nation is Ed Jaksha of Nebraska. A World War I Signal Corps veteran, former telephone company manager, and real estate broker, Jaksha was no novice in petition campaigns. On taxes and spending he had been involved for a third of a century, when he took on term limits in 1991. He is both a Republican and a maverick.

Jaksha was President of the Fremont Chamber of Commerce in 1959 when he wrote, and the other members subscribed to, the "Declaration of Independence from Federal Dependence." The precise issue was a proposed federal subsidy for the Fremont Airport. The overall issue was, as Ed put it, "local officials will get reelected forever by passing out other people's money gotten from the federal government."

This Declaration received national attention. Ed was invited to Washington to present the Declaration to President Eisenhower. Due to a scheduling problem, it was accepted by Vice President Nixon. This background led Ed naturally into the term limits effort. Many of the same people who had joined him in forming the Nebraska Taxpayers Association in 1980, joined him for term limits in 1991.

There was no single, leading political opponent of term limits in Nebraska. Governor Ben Nelson, a Democrat, was nominally opposed, but did not fight hard against the initiative since he, like the auditor of public accounts, was already limited to two terms. Governor Nelson, as Ed said, "was good at skating around the issue."

State Auditor John Breslow, also a Democrat, not only supported term limits but served on Jaksha's Advisory Committee for Measure 407, as it became known when it made the ballot.

The major "public" official to oppose term limits was Tom Osborne, coach of the mighty Nebraska football team. He took time in press conferences on football to attack term limits as causing the "loss of good people," and "eliminating institutional memory." Apparently he did so at the behest of the president and the chancellor of the University of Nebraska, both heavily dependent on the largess of the Nebraska Senate.

Cases in other states have established that public officials who use taxpayers' money to take sides on initiative issues clearly violate the First Amendment. However, no action was taken against Coach Osborne.

The two main organizations in opposition were the Nebraska Education Association (the statewide teachers union) and the unicameral Nebraska legislature. Measure 407 placed limits on both members of Congress and all state officials at two terms, except the US House, which would be allowed four terms or eight years. In the middle of the petition campaign, the Nebraska Senate passed an "emergency" law to take effect immediately to prevent petition gatherers from working across county lines. Because Nebraska has 93 counties, many quite small, this law would have destroyed the effort.

The Attorney General, Don Stenberg, agreed this was a serious assault on the rights of Nebraskans on this or any other petition subject. He took the new law to court. Within three weeks the Nebraska Supreme Court agreed, and struck the law down.

In November 1992, 481,000 Nebraskans voted for term limits, a margin of 68 to 32 percent in favor. But the story does not end there. In 1994 the Nebraska Supreme Court ruled, in a challenge by opponents of term limits, that the secretary of state had told limit supporters the wrong number of petitions to file. It was, the court opined, 91,000 rather than the 59,000 the secretary of state had set. The court threw out the results of the 1992 election.

So, Ed Jaksha hiked up his pants and got to work again. The people of Nebraska were upset over their decision being thrown away. As many people said to Ed in signing new petitions, "Last time I didn't take a position, but by God, this time I'm for you." There were 132,000 signatures filed. Limits will be on the Nebraska ballot and will probably pass by an even wider margin this time.

Sherry Bockwinkel, Skip Cook, and Ed Jaksha are just three of the thousands of Americans who have taken leadership positions in the term limits effort. They are quite different from one another in age, style, background and politics. But they share several common qualities. Most term limits leaders are novices in politics. (Jaksha is an exception, with his background in petition campaigns.) All find themselves opposed by powerful and well-funded organizations, and by powerful and entrenched politicians.

It is a typical David and Goliath situation. And, in term limits, as in the Biblical story, the little guy wins. Some press reports have said, wrongly, that term limit supporters are better funded than their opponents because of strong financial support from US Term Limits for state efforts. In most cases, supporters have been outspent by opponents. Even in the few cases where the funds have been equal or limits supporters have had more money, the battle has not been equal as election day approaches. The reason is that supporters must spend much of their money on the mechanics of getting petitions, and often on litigation to defend their efforts against assault.

Ironically, opponents of term limits have sought to portray supporters as Goliath and themselves as David. They do this by pointing out the tens of thousands of dollars that supporters raise early, some of it from out of state. But, they don't mention the high costs of operating a petition campaign, which supporters must do while the opposition waits to see if the issue will even make it onto the ballot.

Additionally, opponents charge that supporters are "well organized" and "massive" while opponents have no organization. Again, supporters have to organize early to comply with petition deadlines. Opponents can wait until the question is certified for the ballot. Then they demonstrate remarkable ability to organize and raise funds in a matter of weeks, much more quickly than the amateurs running the prolimits campaigns.

As Paul Jacob, Executive Director of US Term Limits, says, opposition efforts are "run right out of congressional offices and public employee union offices." On the ability of opponents to get organized when they choose to, he noted that opposing special interests "are among the most organized operations in the country, some of them for forty years or more."

In short, opponents can say whatever they want about limits supporters early in the campaign when supporters are scrambling for signatures. When the rubber hits the road in September and October for the general election, supporters are David and opponents are Goliath.

This happens state after state except where the professional politicians see poll numbers as high as 75 percent in support of limits. Then they recognize that nothing will defeat limits at the polls. So they don't campaign for no votes on the initiative. They lurk in the bushes waiting to file suit to throw out the results after the election.

In the last two months before most initiative elections, opponents outspend supporters by 2 to 1 in TV commercials on term limits. Opponents rely on political professionals who produce slick spots repeating the attacks of the Foley Forces. Supporters must rely primarily on free media — press reports on the issue and the campaigns.

For the most part, the press has been fair in its coverage. Occasionally, it will attack supporters over the nature of the people who donate money to them. Less often will the press ferret out the sources for, and reasons for, contributions to opponents.

Occasionally, the press will portray supporters as nuts and flakes and opponents as responsible and thoughtful types. But more often, the press will describe both sides for who they are and what they are, state the issue, and let the chips fall where they may. That is more than enough, since public outrage about nonresponsive, entrenched incumbents is sufficient to carry term limits to success almost every time they appear on the ballot.

The supporters of term limits are a varied and colorful lot. The major, national organizations are Americans to Limit Congressional Terms, Americans Back in Charge, and US Term Limits. The last is by far the largest, best funded, best staffed and most effective. The winner for the most colorful name, however, is L.I.M.I.T.S. — Let Incumbents Mosey into the Sunset — founded by Frank Eisenzimmer in Oregon.

Though L.I.M.I.T.S. is an interesting name, the implication is incorrect. Incumbents almost never "mosey" into the sunset. They either are pushed into it, kicking and screaming about their unjust fate, or go quietly in a mahogany box with six bronze handles.

> ***The Incumbent's Motto***
>
> They'll get me out of Congress when they unwrap my cold, dead fingers from my electronic voting card.

The term limit movement has gone further, with more successes in a short period of time, than any other reform movement in American history. Limits have succeeded in 15 states in two years, far more in that time than accomplished by women's suffrage, the direct election of US senators, or any other change that began at the state level. With that rapid growth came difficulties.

The first initiative in Washington State was retroactive. Terms already served before the initiative was approved would have counted toward the limits. That initiative, 553, lost in 1991 by a margin of 54-46 percent. Also, it applied limits to statewide elected officials, as well as to members of Congress.

Exit polls of voters in that election confirmed that the retroactive provision was the killer. The people did not want most major politicians in the state to be forced out as of the very next election. On the other hand, popular support for term limits in the future was quite strong.

Learning from a narrow loss, Bockwinkel's organization, the Washington LIMITS Campaign, made the new initiative, 573, prospective only. It counts against the limit on terms served only those *after* the law went into effect. With that change, term limits passed in 1992, by a margin of 52–48 percent.

A conference on term limits was held in San Jose, California, in December 1991. In attendance were volunteers and activists from more than half the states. The first defeat in Washington State in 1991 was compared to the first victory in Colorado in 1990. Each state campaign was independent; although many leaders of the effort wanted term limits in effect now, not six or twelve years from now, all the petitioners for 1992 decided to go with prospective language only.

Also, because the state by state efforts were independent of one another, the definitions of the precise nature of term limits varied across the country.

Term limits come in two basic flavors, lifetime limits and length–of–service limits. The former bar anyone from serving in that office again after the maximum terms, as with the 22nd Amendment restricting presidents to two terms in office. Length–of–service restrictions require an incumbent to leave office for a period of time before running for it again.

The latter restriction uses two methods, an outright ban or a requirement that the incumbent cannot have his name printed on the official ballot but can still run a write–in campaign. Very few people have ever been elected to federal office with write–in campaigns. Proponents of these laws believe they have a better chance of Supreme Court approval than outright bans. The author, a Supreme Court practitioner, believes the outcome of the test case will be broader and will not turn on whether the ban is outright or just a matter of ballot access. (See Chapter 10.)

Other differences are primarily whether the House is restricted to three, four or six terms, meaning six, eight or 12 years in office. Most limits are three terms or six years. The longest one is in Colorado (six terms, 12 years); that may be reduced to three terms and six years in 1994.

When the term limit effort first began, the supporters had no idea how eager people would be to sign their petitions. They had no idea what sort of contributions would come in, and no idea how popular the idea would be.

At the same time, the public's views among those who supported term limits had not yet jelled around the preferred limits for the US House. The changing of American public opinion on limits over the last generation and its coalescing around the three–term (six–year) limit for the House are discussed in Chapter 3.

In short, the growing pains for term limits included differences between the various jurisdictions on the definitions of the limits to be applied, and how to apply them. This was not merely a result of different opinions among the leaders of the limits effort; it also reflected different opinions among the people. Now that the term limits movement has matured, public opinion has solidified. There are fewer differences among initiatives today. The nearly universal pattern now is "3 and 2 Plan," three terms in the House, two terms in the Senate. For state and local officials, it is two terms for almost all offices, three if the term length is just two years.

There is a long, hard process between the design of the initial petition and the success of the law or constitutional amendment in the next general election. In the first Washington State campaign, the Foley Forces did not take the initiative seriously until late in the campaign. Then they conducted some public opinion polls that showed the same results as independent ones conducted by the press; retroactive term limits were headed for a major victory.

The Foley Forces then pulled out most of the stops. They conducted heavy fundraising and blitzed supporters with slick

TV ads claiming that Washington state water would be diverted to California, the state would lose federal benefits, etc.

In the 1992 rematch, each side knew to take the other seriously from the beginning. Sherry Bockwinkel knew the high level of support for term limits among the people. Speaker Foley knew that limits would win unless he could force the genie back into the bottle.

By 1992, Speaker Foley recognized this was not just an isolated rebellion by some voters in his state, but also an effort with national implications. He did not realize, perhaps does not realize to this day, the strength and permanence of this effort.

Foley knows he can get reelected anytime he wants in his Spokane district. He knows that Congressman Dan Rostenkowski, the extreme example, can win again in Chicago despite being under indictment for 17 felonies. So can Congressman McDade in Pennsylvania, despite his indictments.

Foley confuses the reelection of incumbents with respect for incumbents or acceptance of the system as it is. Having made that mistake, he assumes that the voters don't really mean it when they vote for term limits.

Perhaps the reelection of Rostenkowski in November 1994 will get the message through to Foley. But even if it gets through, Foley is unlikely to admit it. The system as it is, including Speaker Foley in Congress for 30 years and counting, is too basic to his belief structure to admit of doubts.

> ***The 1994 Poster Child for Term Limits***
>
> Danny Rostenkowski will always win in his Chicago House district, as long as he's still breathing and not currently incarcerated. That's why he has been named the 1994 Poster Child for Term Limits.

The two Washington state campaigns illustrated that all political campaigns, not just for candidates, depend on fundraising for much of their success. Napoleon said, "An army marches on its stomach." To the same effect, political campaigns march on their wallets.

Table A in the Technical Appendix gives examples of major contributors ($5,000 and up) that oppose term limits. It also analyzes reasons why corporations and special interests donate large sums of money to oppose an issue which doesn't seem to have any relevance to them.

One of the fascinations about contributions by term limits opponents is why they are made. Why does a top–drawer law firm in New York City contribute to a state initiative in Michigan? Why does a utility that does business in Southern California contribute money a thousand miles from home?

Major corporations are conspicuous by their presence on this list. If, like the wide majority of all Americans, you support term limits, are you concerned that corporations which put breakfast food on your table, or beer in your refrigerator, or programs on your television are dumping money into campaigns around the country to defeat what you want?

Various public service unions plus the aerospace workers (who are private, but depend on public money) are heavily involved, with free volunteers and cash money in these vote–no campaigns. Do they think long–term Congressmen like John Dingell of Michigan will spend other people's money like water in order to keep the unions happy? Do they fear that new members of Congress who would win after term limits kick in will listen more to the taxpayers, who demand that government be more competent and efficient in using the public's money? Do they think the new congressmen will be harder to control?

When congressional campaign offices, including offices of candidates from other states, show up as contributors to defeat an out–of–state initiative, what message are they giving? Is it just I'll scratch your back, you scratch mine, among long–term incumbents all over the country? Do the individuals who donated money to support candidates for election know that their money is being siphoned off not for an election campaign, but to defeat the will of the voters in initiatives in other states?

None of this flow of money into the coffers of term limit opponents is illegal. All the major contributions (over $5,000) shown in Table A; came from public records in various states that require reporting of initiative campaign donors. However, it may be an eye–opening experience to the public to see what is going on. Major corporations around the country are being leaned on by powerful incumbents in Congress to cough up the greenies. To their discredit, they are complying promptly with fat checks. Perhaps their millions of customers might want to suggest that these retail corporations change their position on term limits.

The leaders of the term limits movement across the board are politically aware, and sometimes politically active, but on issues rather than candidates. They support the idea of citizen–legislators at all levels of government, not just Congress.

The civic attitudes of term limits activists are similar to those behind the progressive and populist movements for political reform at the turn of the century. They are also similar to the thinking of the delegates who gathered in Philadelphia in 1787 to write the US Constitution. (For an introduction to the Framers' views on term limits, see Chapter 5.)

The leaders of the opposition are the opposite. They are either career politicians or close associates of career politicians. They believe that government is too important to be left to "amateurs," that only long–term politicians have the knowledge and the experience to guide the federal government.

Both sides represent only political theory. Reality time comes when the voters hear the arguments of both sides and make their sovereign judgment.

At the beginning of the term limit movement for Congress, the issue was in public doubt. Today it is not. The public has decided that long–time incumbency should not be tolerated. And the only real weapon the incumbents have left to protect themselves and their perks is a parade of lawsuits intended to overturn the judgments of their own people.

2

Congress for Life?

The Problem of Careerism in Congress

For the first 125 years of American history under its new Constitution, we were governed by citizen representatives in Congress and in the White House. Tradition, not legal requirements, maintained this condition.

Presidents followed the example of George Washington, who served two terms as president and then went home, not because he was forced to but because he believed in "rotation in office." That meant elected leaders would not always remain in office, but would in turn be the governed, rather than the rulers.

In 1940, President Franklin Delano Roosevelt broke that tradition by running for and winning a third term, and then a fourth. The nation responded by adopting the 22nd Amendment in 1951, providing that no person shall serve as president more than two terms. All presidents since then have been required by law, rather than encouraged by George Washington's example, to serve limited terms.

A similar, less noticed change was occurring in Congress at the same time. The tradition there was that members would serve perhaps two terms in the House, one or maybe two in the Senate, and then return to their homes to live under the laws they had written.

For our first 125 years, about 35 percent of the members of the House retired before every election. They were not usually faced with potential defeat if they chose to run again. These were "voluntary quits," members who went home because they believed that was good for them and good for the nation.

This does not mean that pure altruism was at work here. In the first century, congressmen had not yet learned the art of feathering their own nests with hundred-thousand-dollar salaries, million–dollar pensions, large and obsequious staffs, and all the perks and privileges that power is heir to. In short, remaining in Congress for decades was not as attractive then as now.

Also, Congress had not yet invented the massive committee structure and the rigorous seniority system to fill the leadership positions. If power, rather than luxury, was to be the draw to keep members coming back, term after term, that was also in short supply in the first century.

Average turnover in the House for the entire first century of our government was 43 percent in *every* election. There were a few convictions or expulsions then, as now, and there were deaths. But almost all of this massive turnover was due to "voluntary quits." See Table B; in the Technical Appendix. To put that statistic in perspective, the highest turnover in any election in the second century was in 1932 during the Great Depression. The landslide that brought FDR into office also caused a turnover in the House of 37.7 percent, still substantially less than the average for all of the prior century.

Today, the press and political "experts" vigorously debate careerism in Congress. Among the people that debate has long since been decided. There is no debate, however, that congressional tenure has sharply increased, especially among the leaders of Congress, in the last 70 years.

There is a common error about *why* this change has occurred. Most reporters and "experts" point to rising reelection rates of incumbents as the basic reason. This is more than half wrong.

Reelection rates have risen, but not sharply. In the first 102 years of our history beginning in 1790 (the second election), the reelection rate in the House was 82.5 percent, overall. In the first 13 elections, 1790–1812, the average reelection rate was a very modern number of 93.7 percent.

In the next 50 years, extending into the 20th century, it was 82.7 percent, overall. In the most recent 52 years it was 90.5 percent, overall. For the entire second 102 years, it was 86.7 percent. So, comparing apples and apples, the reelection rate in the second 51 House elections was only 4.2 percent higher than in the first 51 elections.

This modest increase in the reelection rate cannot account for the large increase in average tenure of congressmen.

The other factor, ordinarily overlooked, is the decline in "voluntary quits." Members who simply decided to go home rather than run again, used to account for more than two–thirds of the turnover in every election. The lack of "voluntary quits" accounts for more than two–thirds of the drastic increase in average tenure.

The graphics on pages 22–23 show these relationships over time. Rising reelection rates *and* declining voluntary quits are both necessary to create the present level of careerism in Congress.

What about the Senate, alert readers will say at this point? First of all, senators were not popularly elected until after the 17th Amendment was adopted in 1913. Before then, they were chosen by each state legislature. Second, elections for Senate are more visible, better funded for challengers to incumbents, and more competitive than House races. The problem of careerism in the Senate is sharply different from that in the House.

Because of the filibuster and points of personal privilege in the Senate and the capacity of any senator to introduce any amendment to almost any bill on the floor, the leaders of the Senate have far less control and influence over the individual senators and especially over the contents of legislation than leaders of the House have over their colleagues and their proposed bills. Likewise, committee chairmen in the Senate have far less power over the contents of legislation, or over the more important point, whether legislation on a particular subject ever reaches the Senate floor.

In the House, the Speaker exercises strong control, sometimes dictatorial control, over what will pass and what will never reach the floor. Committee chairmen exercise similar control in the subject areas of their various committees. So, the House is less democratic both in the election of its members, and in the ability of its rank and file members to accomplish anything legislatively, once they get to Washington.

The Foley Forces are fond of saying that "high" turnover in 1992 demonstrates that term limits are unnecessary. The first error in that assertion is the turnover rate of 25.3 percent was not high by historical standards. Only the exceptionally low turnover rates in the last two decades make it seem "high." The second error is that turnover rates are always atypical in years ending with a "2." This is due to the ten–year cycle of "partial incumbency."

The Constitution requires a national census every ten years, from 1790. So, the House has been reapportioned every ten years, from 1792. Reapportionment causes incumbents to run against other incumbents. In five races in 1992 that virtually ensured five incumbents would win, and five would lose.

More commonly, reapportionment adds areas to incumbents' districts that they never represented before. They face voters who don't know them from Adam. In those areas — sometimes a substantial portion of the new district — the incumbent lacks the advantages of incumbency and is just another name on the ballot. In short, every ten years when House districts increase in size due to national population growth, incumbents become partial incumbents.

Turnover in the House, 1790–1890

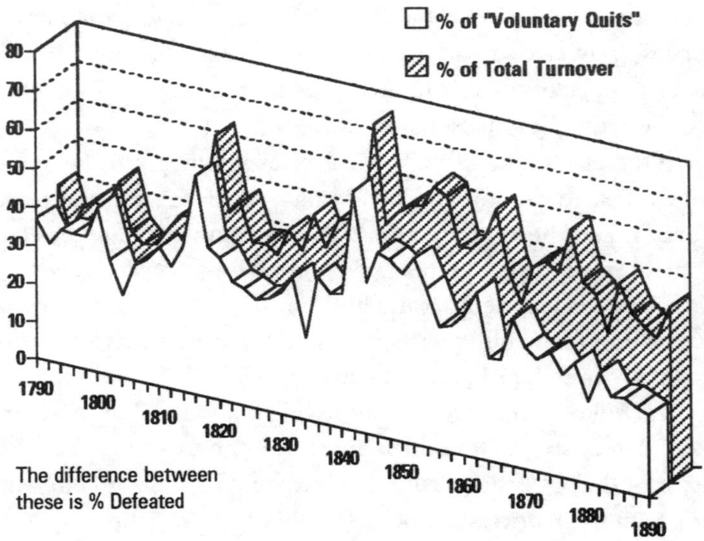

This, in turn, draws more and stronger challengers into the races. The goal of gerrymandering, whether done by Republicans or Democrats, is to make seats stronger for the more influential incumbents, meaning those with most seniority and clout. So, long–term incumbents get districts with higher proportions of voters in their party. That makes them safer in the general election. But in redistricting years only, it makes them more vulnerable in party primaries.

History demonstrates the special nature of these years. In every decade since 1932, more incumbents have been defeated in their party primaries in redistricting years than in any other elections. As noted before, 1932 was a watershed year in

American politics when FDR swept into office. An all–time record of 42 incumbents were denied renomination. But the pattern continued in normal redistricting years. In 1942, 20 incumbents lost in their primaries. In 1952, 9 lost. In 1962, 12 lost. In 1972, it was 12 again. In 1982, 10 lost in primaries.

Turnover in the House, 1892–1992

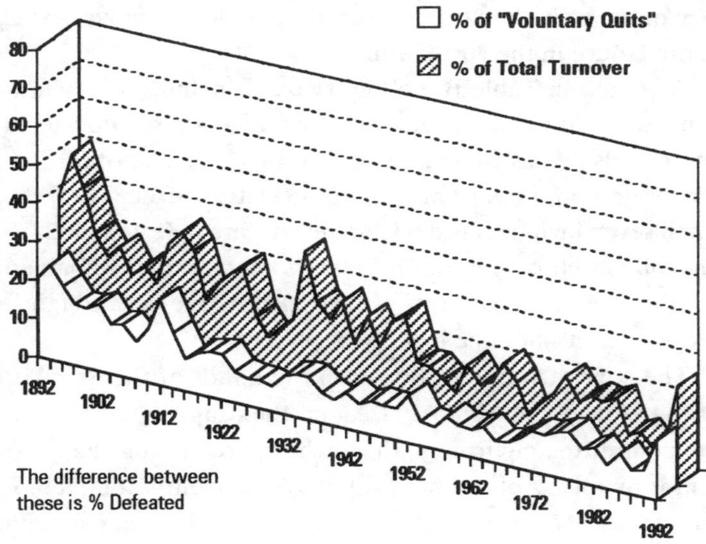

The number of incumbents defeated in their own primaries in 1992 was 19. Low though this is by historical standards, it will probably be the highest rate for this decade.

Redistricting has another effect, which also applies in all years ending in a "2." It causes some incumbents to assess their positions and decide to retire or run for other offices, rather than seek reelection to the House. Elective defeat is not now, and never has been, the primary cause of turnover in the House. The primary reason has been voluntary quits.

The graphics on pages 22–23 show the trends in reelection and voluntary quits from 1790 to 1992. Until 1900, there were only two years in which the voluntary quit rate was *below* 15 percent (1808 and 1870). Since 1902, there has only been one year in which the voluntary quit rate rose *above* 15 percent (1912). The effect has been most pronounced in the 27 elections beginning in 1938. In all but five of those, the voluntary quit rate has been less than 10 percent. (The exceptions are 1952, and 1972–78.). This one major change, declining voluntary quits, is the key to the exceptionally low turnover rates in the House in the 20th century.

As noted in Table B, voluntary quits includes all incumbents who did not run again. So, this category picks up deaths and expulsions as well as choices not to run. The other factors are not an important part of the statistic except in 1988, when seven incumbents died and seven were defeated. Still, 26 incumbents chose not to run again. Voluntary quits remained in 1988 the main cause of House turnover, even though it dropped to its all–time low of 7.6 percent.

The concentration of power in the hands of the Speaker of the House, the Majority Leader, the Majority Whip, and the committee chairmen, all of whom are among the most senior members of the majority party (currently the Democrats), has a second effect — reinforcing high careerism and low turnover. Most special interests in Washington, especially those which raise and spend the most money on congressional elections, are organized according to the economic interests they represent.

In 1992, the ten largest Political Action Committees (PACs) in total dollars given to candidates for the House, were: Realtors, at $2.95 million; American Medical Assoc., $2.94; Teamsters, $2.44; Trial Lawyers, $2.37; Nat'l Education Assoc. (teachers union), $2.32; United Auto Workers, $2.23; AFSCME (public employee union), $1.95; Nat'l Automobile Dealers, $1.78; Nat'l Rifle Assoc., $1.74; and the Letter Carriers, $1.71 million.

Using a chart of House committees, one easily sees the committees these PACs look to for legislation in their favor, or for blockage of legislation which might harm them. The Realtors look to banking and commerce, the doctors to all committees dealing with health care, the Teamsters to labor and commerce. They win the Mom–flag–and–apple–pie award for their PAC name. It doesn't mention "Teamsters." It's the "Democratic, Republican, Independent Voter Education Committee."

Where do these special interests concentrate their money, and why? They give dominantly to incumbent congressmen who serve on their committees of interest. Plus, they give heavily to the top leaders, Speaker Foley, Majority Leader Richard Gephardt of Missouri, and Majority Whip David Bonior.

Special interests also give heavily to "leadership PACs" organized by such officials. A leadership PAC is a cash drawer controlled by a leader to accept far more money than that person possibly needs for reelection. The leader then parcels the money out to rank and file members of his party who need it. The recipients then become loyal supporters of whatever the leader wants in the future.

This song and dance with leadership PACs was one of the reasons why a former Speaker of the House, Jim Wright of Texas, was forced to resign from the House while under investigation, and why a former Majority Whip, Tony Coehlo of California, resigned rather than face an investigation (rumored, but not yet begun when he left).

In short, PACs know which side their bread is buttered on, and they give money on that basis. PACs gave 71.7 percent to incumbents in 1992 (only 11.7 percent to challengers). They did not neglect the Republicans. Minority Leader Robert Michel and Minority Whip Newt Gingrich of Georgia received smaller donations, but still much more than rank and file members.

Again, the logic of the special interests is clear. The Republicans *might* gain the majority after the election, and if they do, Michel's successor (he has announced his retirement) and Gingrich's successor (he seems poised to take Michel's position) will be Speaker and Majority Whip, respectively.

> ***The Damon Runyon Cover***
>
> Special interests give money to incumbents per the Damon Runyon Cover: "The race is not always to the swift nor the battle to the strong, but that's the way to bet."

PACs understand most major legislation does not pass today without *some* Republican support. Supporting leaders of the minority party is good business — not as good as supporting majority leaders — but, an insurance policy, nonetheless.

So, consideration of careerism in the House should focus on its leadership, separate from its rank and file members. The committee chairmen usually decide whether a bill on any subject reaches the floor at all, and if so, what its major provisions will be — and which provisions will be left on the cutting room floor. The Speaker appoints the members of the Rules Committee, and that committee writes the conditions under which any bill reaches the floor. Often it writes a "closed rule," meaning that other than chosen and stated amendments, no amendments can be offered by anyone on the floor of the House.

Provisions like the closed rule are particularly appreciated by special interests that know how to navigate the halls of power in Washington but know that their interests are not popular with the people back home. A closed rule means no grandstanding freshman congressman can offer an amendment on the floor that will gut–shoot the deal they have carefully worked out.

The graphic on the following page shows both the change in average tenure of the rank and file members of the House of Representatives. It is prepared from Table C in the Technical Appendix.

Average Tenure, House of Representatives, 1952–90

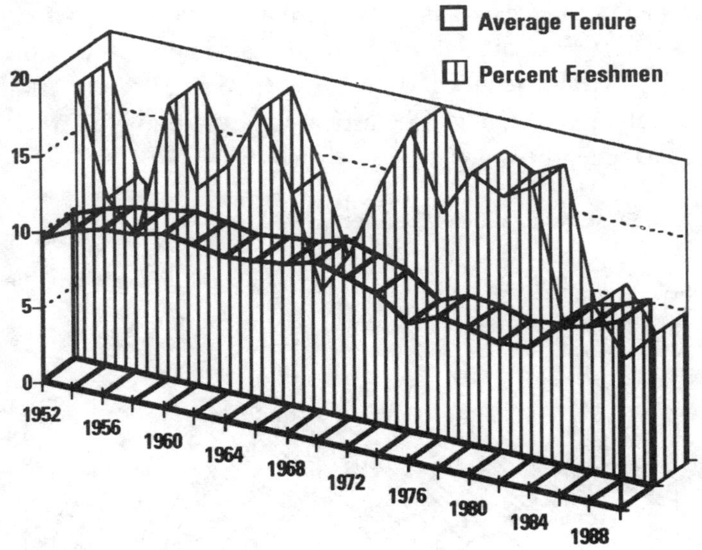

There are 28 major leadership positions in the House — the Speaker, Majority Leader, Majority Whip (Democrats), Minority Leader, Minority Whip (Republicans), and the 23 committee chairmanships (all Democrats). These are the standing committees of the House, plus the Permanent Select Committee on Intelligence. The Intelligence Committee was included because it is "permanent." Other select and joint committees were not included. Tenure of all these leaders turned out to be almost equal to tenure of the five top leaders. Using just the Democratic and Republican leaders avoids a bias in favor of either party over time.

The graphics above and on the following page (based on Table D) compare the average tenure of the whole House with the leaders who control most of its work and output.

Members of Congress tend to have their political philosophies fairly well established by the time they run for and win seats in the House. The average member was first elected when

President George Bush was elected in 1988. By contrast, the average House *leader* was first elected when President Richard Nixon came into office in 1968. To put that in perspective, the average House leader has been in office since the original Woodstock Art and Music Festival took place in New York, a quarter century ago.

Average Tenure, House Leaders, 1900–94

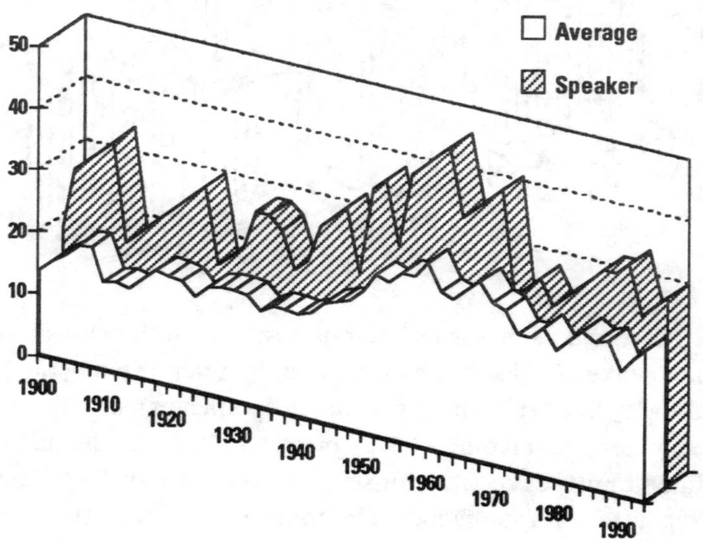

It is the leadership, and the seniority system that places the oldest members in the positions of greatest power, that poses the greatest danger to the operation of the House. The degree to which the leadership, and therefore the legislative output of the House, are out of touch with the American people, arises from how long ago any of the leaders faced a truly competitive election. Absent competition, the leaders need only pay lip service, not close attention, to the views of their constituents.

Even today, when dissatisfaction with Congress is at its height and an anti–incumbent fever is also high, according to all national public opinion polls, it will still be true in November that about 25 percent of all incumbents will run without major party challengers. In the past, about 30 percent of all Democrat incumbents ran without opposition and 25 percent of the Republican ones. This year, the Republicans are making a special effort to give no Democrat a free ride.

The critical question, however — the biennial deception in which the press plays a major role — is the difference between a name on the ballot and an opponent who has any real chance of success. Every incumbent who has any paper challenger in a primary or general election will repeatedly comment that "Smith is a serious challenger. He/she is running a good race."

The incumbent doesn't mean a word of it. The author has present or former members of Congress as personal friends. They or their administrative assistants (their alter egos) have sometimes stated they have no concern whatever about an overwhelming victory over their next opponent. He won't embarrass those who have spoken candidly by quoting them. The Foley Forces certainly have similar conversations with their friends.

The truth is, experienced incumbents know full well the difference between a challenger who represents a real threat and those who are just passing names on meaningless ballots. All incumbents in such walk–over elections use the Lou Holtz Bluff.

> ***The Lou Holtz Bluff***
>
> Always refer to your opponent in an election as a serious potential threat. Even if you are as certain as Lou Holtz at Notre Dame that you will pound your opponent into the mud by halftime, never say such a thing no matter how true it is.

All experienced incumbents know a dirty little truth — *most House elections are over six months to a year before they are held.* Experienced members of the press know the same thing, but they dare not report it. Conflict sells newspapers and gets people to watch TV. And that, in turn, sells cars, beer, and underarm deodorant. If there isn't any real conflict in congressional races, false conflict will do just as well as long as the public hasn't caught on.

Those are bold charges. They can be proved.

Prediction of House Races Using June 1994 Financial Data

On June 21, 1992, an article this author co–wrote with Edward Roeder of Sunshine Press, Washington, was published in the *Orlando Sentinel.* That article predicted all but 5 percent of the House races for November. Despite the fact it was a redistricting year and assorted scandals were underfoot such as the House Bank scandal, the House Post Office scandal (coming soon to a courtroom near you), the predictions were 96.7 percent accurate. Back in June, we predicted 110 freshmen in the House; there were 110 freshmen, come November. On freshmen, we missed two races each way, so our total was correct but our calls were not 100 percent right.

To prove the charges just made, this book predicts 95.4 percent of the House races for November 1994, using data as of June 13, 1994. Only two criteria were used to make these predictions, money and incumbency. Issues are ignored. Personalities are ignored. Votes for or against President Clinton on the budget, NAFTA, gun control, abortion, or any other subject, are ignored. Nothing but money and incumbency of candidates and parties was considered.

The predictions, state by state, and district by district within each state, appear in Table E; in the Technical Appendix. Each prediction shows this information — the party expected to win, the candidate expected to win (and whether he/she is an incumbent) and the strength of prediction. Categories of prediction are: 3 = moral certainty of victory; 2 = high probability; 1 = expected victory. Only 4.6 percent of the races, just two involving incumbents, are rated as tossups.

In the 18 open–seat races rated as tossups, there will be a Republican landslide. So, 60 percent of these were assigned to Republicans. Here are the high (or low) points of the results:

1. The Democrats will retain control of House, 248—187, plus or minus four seats.
2. The number of freshmen in the House will be 53, give or take three. Turnover will be 12.5 percent.
3. Both Congressmen under felony indictments, McDade (R, Pa., 10th) and Rostenkowski (D, Ill., 5th) will be reelected.
4. The House incumbent reelection rate will rise again, to 98 percent ± 0.5, close to its all–time high in 1988.
5. Almost all open–seat elections (no incumbent running) will be won by the candidate raising the larger total of money.
6. The only independent or third–party winner will be Sanders (I, Vt.).
7. Most victors will win by a landslide, which is defined as a margin of 55—45 or better. (That corresponds to President Lyndon Johnson in 1964 and Ronald Reagan in 1980.)
8. No network or print media political experts will match the level of accuracy of these predictions until they have data after Labor Day. Then, they will offer tortured explanations why their prior predictions were in error.
9. These predictions will be at least 97.5 percent accurate.

How can predictions like these be made so long before the election? The reason is, history demonstrates that modern House elections are decided by dollars, not votes. The equation is a simple one: power = money = media = reelection. The equation is also circular. Reelection means more seniority, which means more power, which means greater certainty of reelection for those with the most terms already served.

The only exception to this rule is that live bodies willing to work in campaigns can to some extent substitute for money. Union support primarily but not exclusively for Democratic incumbents is reflected not just in donations from union PACs, but also in the commitment of members to work in campaigns of favored incumbents. But, other than that, money is the sole determining factor.

Incumbency is reflected in money, since the special interests bet heavily, by ratios of 8–1 up to 11–l on incumbents. The logic is straightforward. The incumbent already has certain power. After the election, he/she will have more power, due to increase in seniority. The incumbent is better than 95 percent likely to win.

Therefore, to be on the right side of a member of a critical committee, or, more important, the chairman of that committee, dig deep and donate now.

> ***Congressional Elections***
> A process to determine who can raise the most money from special interest groups.

If a heavy–set man with no neck and a cheap suit enters your dry cleaning store and demands money so your shop won't burn down, that's called extortion. It is illegal. If a well–dressed, well–spoken congressional chairman with the power to shut down your whole industry sidles up to you at a cocktail party and asks for a "contribution" to his next campaign, that's called politics. Not only is it legal, the Federal Election Campaign Act requires that the contribution be publicly reported to the penny, with details on the donors.

If money is so important in congressional elections today, why hasn't that always been true? The reasons have to do with district size and the nature and cost of broadcast media.

Please bear with a slight dose of history. When the House of Representatives was first established, each district represented 30,000 people, or about the size of a city council district in a medium–sized city today. This number of citizens is a “shoe–leather” district. A candidate with good qualifications who is attractive to the voters, can meet personally enough people in such a district to win the election, if he/she is perceived as a better choice than the opponent, even if the opponent is an incumbent.

That doesn’t make money totally irrelevant in shoe–leather districts. Some money has to be spent for gas, staff pizzas, lawn signs, bumper stickers, postage, and coffee and doughnuts for the volunteers. But that kind of money can be raised from friends and neighbors.

In a shoe–leather district, a candidate can tell every known special interest to go pound sand, and still win — if his/her personal qualifications and efforts are good enough.

The equation is quite different in districts of 585,000 which House ones have become. These are “media districts.” A candidate combining the qualities of Abraham Lincoln, Florence Nightingale and Dr. Martin Luther King would have zero chance to win in such a district without hundreds of thousands of dollars to pay for a media campaign. Media campaigns, including expensive 30–second spots on TV, are the only way today to reach the majority of the voters in such a district.

Media costs are roughly comparable to district size, though TV advertising costs are increasing faster than inflation. This money has to come from somewhere; the standard source is special interest contributions.

> ***Special Interest Organization***
> Any organization which understands Congress is a candy machine — insert the right coins, pull the right levers, get the goodies you seek.

The graphic on the following page is based on Table F. It shows trends in three critical elements in congressional races, district size, average cost of a successful campaign, and average percent raised from PACs for such campaigns. The three elements are interrelated.

District size drives the need for media spending, and for total spending. This drives the need to obtain PAC money to pay for all this. And, as noted, PACs bet on probable winners, which means they bet on incumbents.

District Size and Average Total Fundraising in Winning Campaigns for Congress, 1976–92

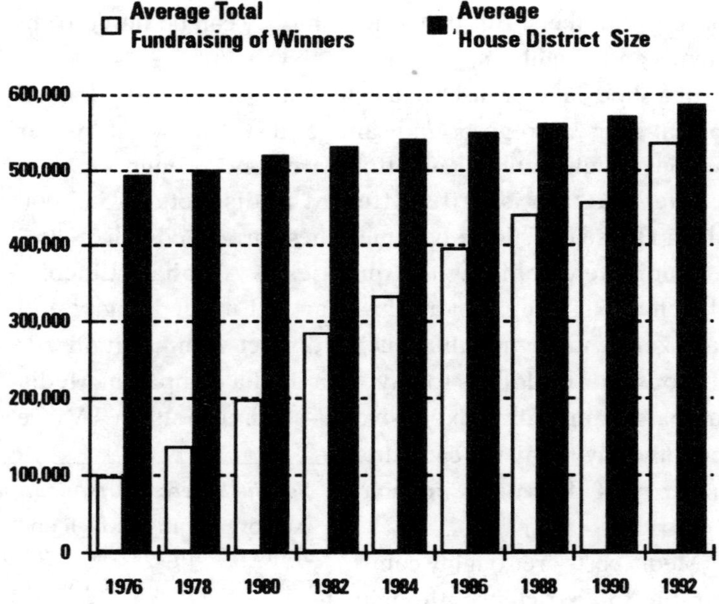

The first use of TV in a presidential campaign was by Dwight D. Eisenhower in 1952. He stood in front of a camera and looked into it occasionally through his spectacles, while he read from a piece of paper he was holding in his hand. By the standards of today's polished TV images, the first political TV commercial was awkward, wooden and dreadful. But then the first car, the first plane, and the first computer were nothing to write home about.

Today, TV spots are a staple in congressional campaigns. Every candidate is searching for the equivalent of the Eveready bunny for his/her TV spots, something to make them stand out amid the clutter of all other political advertising plus ongoing commercial advertising in election years.

> ***The Special Interest Tilt***
>
> Special interests donate 90% of their money to incumbents, because 95% of incumbents win, because special interests donate 90% of their money.... [You get the idea.]

A classic example of a successful TV commercial was by Congressman Lewis, who won the by–election to replace the late Congressman Natcher (D, Ky., 2nd). The technique used was "morphing," changing one face fluidly into another — best known in films like *The Terminator* and *The Abyss.*

The voice–over announcer said, "If you like Clinton, you'll love Prather." As the text changed to taxes and other subjects, the Democrat Prather's face changed into Clinton's and back again. The Republican won handily.

> ***The Television Conclusion***
>
> The relationship of television to election to Congress is explained in the Latin phrase "televisero ergo vici," which means, "I am televised, therefore I win."
>
> (apologies to Russell Baker)

Techniques like that cost money, lots of it, even before the airtime is paid for. That brings us back to the subject of money and prediction of races based on money.

In the last 1,800 races for the House of Representatives, only three challengers to incumbents have won while spending less than $250,000 — Peter Hoekstra (R, Mich., 2nd), Scott Klug (R, Wis., 2nd), and William Orton (D, Utah, 3rd). Circumstances unique to each of those elections critically weakened their opponents or strengthened them, allowing them to beat such huge odds against success. Such circumstances arise very seldom and are totally unpredictable, but they affect less than one race per election, on average.

In short, there is a dollar minimum to make any candidate electable. If the candidate doesn't "make the nut" as owners of retail shops well understand — doesn't raise that minimum amount of money — then it is the same as if he/she never got on the ballot. Such candidates are worse than marginal; they are dead meat from the beginning.

Therefore, the first part of making the predictions involved identifying the candidates who were beyond hope, financially. Because of inflation, the basic amount needed to have a chance has increased. For 1994 the minimum amount to beat an incumbent in a general election will be about $350,000. The total amount for the two–year cycle 1993–94 was projected from amounts reported as required by law to the Federal Election Commission as of June 13, 1994. Candidates with primaries before June 25 had to report by June 13. All others had to report as of March 31.

Any challenger running against an incumbent with less money than needed for a competent campaign was counted out. Then any challenger with the basic amount, but still less than half as much as the incumbent, was also counted out. The only way a challenger was predicted to win against an incumbent was if he/she raised at least 50 percent more than the incumbent — Michael Huffington (R, Calif., 22nd) spent $5,443,000 to take an incumbent's seat in 1992. He did that by putting up mostly his own money. Perhaps five House challengers will significantly outspend incumbents in 1994. Of those five, three are likely to win, two more have a chance.

The Proxmire–Whitten Exception

It has been reported that former Senator Proxmire and retiring Congressman Whitten won reelection bids while spending less than $25. Well–entrenched incumbents can do that. This equation is not reversible in favor of challengers.

Predicting open–seat races is trickier, since there is a track record of candidates with less money winding up as the victor, unlike the history of challengers to incumbents. The same basic rule was applied. Any candidate with less than $350,000 in projected total fundraising was counted out at the beginning. Then, ratios were used, with open–seat candidates with less than half their opponents' amounts being counted out.

Once the lower amount for an open seat was within 80 percent of the higher amount, money alone could no longer predict the outcome. At that point, the incumbent party became a consideration. Once all those factors were used for all races in November, a total of 18 races remained unpredicted. These are listed as tossups.

Two elements remain to be discussed. One is the natural advantage that incumbents have, from free mail via the franking privilege, use of Congress's studios to prepare and send out TV and radio pieces for news use, and the general use of staff, expenses and facilities not just to function as the incumbent congressman, but to guarantee high name recognition, which is the first big mountain any challenger must climb before anything else can be done in his/her campaign. Of course it is illegal for congressmen to use their staffs to assist their reelection bids, but anyone who thinks that doesn't happen is welcome to invest in a bridge in Brooklyn.

> ***Congressional Challenger***
>
> Anyone who has a year of time and $250,000 to waste, and holds the vain belief that congressional elections are fair and competitive.

The other open element is the possibility of reforming congressional elections by some mechanism other than term limits, so races become competitive again. Most commonly, the "reformers" who oppose term limits assert that other reforms such as campaign finance reform could accomplish the purpose without the liabilities of term limits. This type of reform is referred to as "leveling the playing field" and involves ensuring that challengers have the same amount of money as incumbents.

The problem with finance reform, however, is the same Congress that benefits from the present situation is the one that would have to pass the reform. Even if theoretically possible, it is impossible in the real world. It's like putting the fox in charge of hen house security.

The first problem is that campaign finance reform is based on public financing of congressional elections. All candidates, incumbents and challengers alike, would be subject to caps on total spending and types of fundraising, if they accept the public financing. (This would parallel the presidential system.) But, the public has made it clear time and again it does not want public financing.

There is a deeper problem. Public financing would be equal for all candidates for Congress. That would put the incumbents at a permanent advantage, because of the various advantages built into the system by incumbents and for incumbents. Political scientists have worked for years to compute the amount of advantage that incumbents have, as an automatic percentage of the vote they have in their pocket, before the polls open. Figures vary from 5 percent to 15 percent for that advantage.

> ***The Level–Playing–Field Test***
>
> Whenever Congress says it has "leveled the playing field," ask whether the incumbents would be willing to switch sides with the challengers. If not, they fail the test.

Assume a middle number between the high and low estimates, say 8 percent as the incumbency benefit. That leaves 92 percent of the vote for the challenger and incumbent to contest. For the challenger to win, he/she must get 50 percent plus one vote. Since the incumbent has 8 percent locked up before the polls open, the challenger must get 54.4 percent of the *available* votes to win. In plain terms, against an

> ***Successful Congressional Challenger***
>
> A challenger already in the race when the incumbent dies, gets sent to jail, or gets written up in *The National Enquirer.*

incumbent, a challenger needs to win the available votes by a landslide, to win the election by a single vote.

That fact, along with the immense fundraising advantages incumbents have, is why incumbents win unless they die, go to jail, or shoot themselves in the foot big–time.

Because of present incumbency advantages, hoping for effective campaign finance reform from the present Congress is vain and can only distract attention from real possibilities for improvement. Congress for life will remain a fact for the foreseeable future, until term limits are established.

> ***Campaign Finance Reform***
>
> Any law that gives the appearance of fairer elections, without seriously compromising the reelection chances of incumbents.

There will be little change in the House of Representatives between this Congress and the next, or between any Congress and the one that follows, unless restraints are placed on the reelection of incumbents for life.

> ***Real* Campaign Finance Reform**
>
> This does not exist. It will *not* exist until more than half of both the House and the Senate have been term–limited.

The Bibliography refers to several books that cover the nature of the perks and privileges, arrogance and absurdities of long–term incumbent congressmen, which is why such tales of woe are not included in this book. Those who like serious commentary in humorous form will particularly enjoy P. J. O'Rourkes's *A Parliament of Whores.* Typical of his lines is this: "Giving money and power to congressmen is like giving whiskey and car keys to teenaged boys."

3

Worse Than Used–Car Salesmen?

The Public's View of Congress

The present attitude of most people about members of Congress is best summed up in this comment, "*They* are no longer like *us.*" Members of Congress pay themselves salaries that are more and more beyond the reach and hopes of average Americans. And they do that by means that are more and more devious.

Congress provides for itself all manner of personal advantages, from multiple gyms to low–cost haircuts, meals, personal goodies, through stores subsidized by the grateful taxpayers. It continually demonstrates its better–than–thou attitude by taking "fact–finding" trips to Jamaica, Hong Kong, and other places where taxpayers would love to go, if they could afford to.

The House Bank may be gone, but special privileges that rub it in go on and on. Every taxpayer who has ever been nailed $20 for bouncing a $11.42 check knows the ignominy and insult. Most of us would love the bank to cheerfully honor our checks with an interest–free overdraft of thousands of dollars. We can't do that for ourselves. But congressmen did it for themselves. That's how the House Bank operated.

In ways both large and small, congressmen continue to demonstrate their belief that they are better than us. Large ways include multi–million–dollar pensions that veteran congressmen have quietly crafted for themselves. Small ways include the special parking lots "for Congress only" that save them from the bane of modern American life, the search for a legal parking space located in the same zipcode as our destination.

> ***The Paycheck Parameter***
>
> Congress blows billions of dollars, the public yawns. Congress kites $100 checks, the public goes ballistic. We don't understand $1 billion; we do understand what fits in our wallet. Here's a translation — a billion dollars is your weekly take–home pay, times all the people in Chicago.

Particularly galling is the fact that congressmen exempt themselves from a host of laws that place additional taxes and regulations on every American business, from giants like General Motors, which have armies of lawyers to fight back, to Mom and Pop grocery stores, cleaners and card shops, which can't fight back and are struggling to survive.

Among the burdens placed on ordinary Americans from which Congress has exempted itself are Acts on Disability, Civil Rights, Age Discrimination, Privacy, Equal Employment, Equal Pay, Minimum Wage, and Social Security, in whole or in part. If these laws are fair and represent good government, why can't Congress live under them? If these laws are intolerable to Congress, why does it place those burdens on us?

The idea that congressmen would become absorbed with possessing and using power and forget where they came from, is not new. The syndrome of "Potomac Fever" was well defined in colonial newspapers by two revolutionary writers using the pseudonym *Cato*. They wrote under pen names because such statements, if directed at agents of King George III, were a hanging offense at the time.

> Men, when they first enter into magistracy,... remember what they themselves suffered with their fellow subjects from the abuse of power, and how much they blamed it; so their first purposes are to be humble, modest and just.... But the possession of power soon alters and vitiates their hearts... by the deceitful incense of false friends and by the prostrate submission of parasites.
>
> First they grow indifferent to all their good designs, then drop them. Next, they lose their moderation. Afterwards, they renounce all measures with their old acquaintance and old principles, and seeing themselves in magnifying glasses, grow in conceit, a different species from their fellow subjects.
>
> And so, by too sudden degrees become insolent, rapacious and tyrannical, ready to catch all means, often the vilest and most oppressive, to raise their fortunes as high as imaginary greatness.

Perhaps this overstates a bit the self–importance of the modern Congress, but not by much. What cure did these revolutionaries offer for the disease of Potomac Fever? "Rotation in office." They concluded, "The only way to put them [Congress] in mind of their former condition, and consequently of the condition of other people, is often to reduce them to it, and to let others of equal capacities share the power in their turn."

For decades, pollsters have been asking Americans to rate the job that Congress is doing between "good," "fair" and "poor." The Gallup Organization asked this question between 1946 and 1958, and Congress got barely tolerable ratings which actually improved over this time span. In April 1946 the ratings were good (14%), fair (42%) and poor (35%). Call it a "gentleman's C." By August 1958 the ratings had become 30%, 42% and only 12% poor. The Roper Polls showed similar results from 1946 to 1983, with ratings in the latter year at 23% excellent/good, 51% fair, and 19% poor.

Starting in 1974 with the Gallup Organization, and spreading to other major polling organizations, the question was changed to "Do you approve of the way Congress is doing its job?" Less than half the times this question was used, it was paired with "Do you approve of the way your congressman is doing his/her job?"

The Gallup results started at 30% yes on Congress, were as high as 47% in the '70s, as high as 42% in the '80s, as high as 40% in the '90s, but dropped to an all–time low of 18% in March 1992. Other major polls showed approval ratings for Congress as high as 54% before the '90s, but all concurred in the recent plummet of that approval. CBS/*New York Times* reported 20% approval of Congress in July 1992. ABC/*Washington Post* showed 16% in June 1992. NBC/*Wall Street Journal* found 15% approval of Congress in April 1992.

Details of these polls are shown in Table G in the Technical Appendix. Continuously from 1974 to 1992, less than half the population approved of Congress. In recent years the numbers of those who approve of Congress have fallen through the floor.

Despite the negative ratings for Congress as an institution, the voters' ratings of their own congressman/woman ran a steady 20%–40% higher. In the same order as described above, these major polls' results on this second question ended as 58% in March 1992, 52% in July 1992, 52% in June 1992, and 55% in April 1992.

The discrepancy between the institutional and individual ratings is explained by most commentators as related to the pork that members bring home to their districts. These projects may be described as boondoggles elsewhere than at home.

They may drive up the deficit. They may even drive up taxes to pay partially, but never fully, for the deficits. Still, it seems the voters want the projects regardless of their national, collective impact on the federal budget. And because of the seniority system that places the longest–serving members of Congress in all the positions of power, they are the ones best able to bring home the pork.

The overall negative view of Congress is confirmed by questions that ask people whether they have "a great deal of confidence" in a list of institutions. In this list, the 1975 responses come first, the 1991 ones are second. These results are from the Gallup Organization. All except the military and television declined in this period. Desert Storm probably explains the rise for the military. Perhaps camcorders and CNN explain the slight rise for television.

Comparative ratings were: Church/Organized Religion, 68%, 56%; Banks/Banking 55%, 29%; Military, 58%, 69%; Public Schools, 56%, 35%; Supreme Court, 49%, 39%; Big Business, 34%, 22%; Television, 21%, 24%; Organized Labor, 38%, 22%; Congress, 40%, 18%; and Newspapers, 51%, 32%.

At the beginning in 1975, Congress was in a moderate position, sixth on the list of ten institutions. At the end in 1991, Congress was dead last on the list. Congress had also lost more than half of its confidence rating in 16 years, the only institution to suffer that badly. Even banks (remember the Savings & Loan crisis?) did not lose as much of their beginning support as did Congress.

Polls other than Gallup's in 1993 give Congress a confidence level of 19%. So, the bottom of the barrel rating for this institution is not temporary. The last time Congress bottomed out in such ratings was in 1990 (remember the House Bank, the House Post Office, the Keating Five in the Senate?). It dropped to 23% in October 1990, according to Gallup. Then, it recovered to an anemic but perhaps tolerable 40% a year later. This time, the descent of Congress to the depths of disapproval seems permanent. It has stayed at or below 20% for two years.

The graphic below charts the change in the approval rating for Congress between 1963 and 1994.

Public Approval of Congress, 1963–94

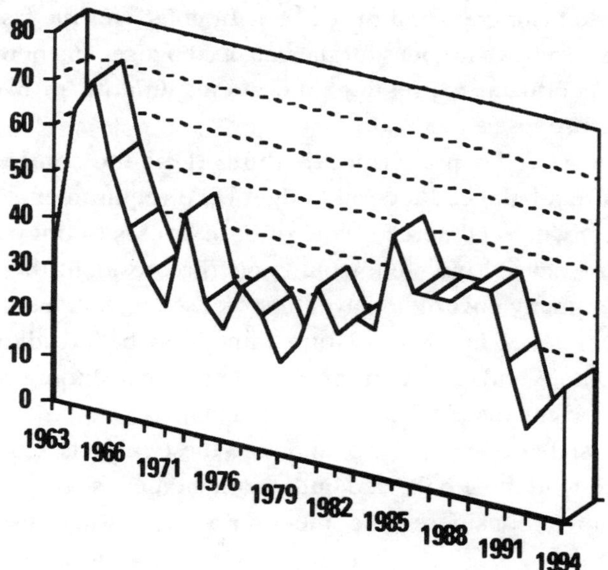

This general bad rating of Congress by the people is not driven solely by the *scandal du jour* in which various members of the House and Senate get caught from time to time. Each of those, as it arrives, causes a separate blip on the radar scope of public opinion. Each may drive the overall rating down several points, but the decreases prior to the 1990s were temporary. In this decade, the decreases are permanent even after the individual scandal is forgotten.

The general disrespect for Congress is also related to the differences between congressional stands on certain issues and those of the public on the same issues. There are at least four issues on which the public stands on one side of the issue, yet the Congress clings to the other.

The proposed balanced budget amendment for the US Constitution, the proposed line–item veto for the president, term limits, and cutting spending rather than raising taxes as the means to close the deficit are all examples of the disparity between Congress and the people. In polls over the last two years (over two decades for the balanced budget amendment), among citizens expressing an opinion, support for each of these proposals was 2 to 1.

By way of explanation, the budget amendment would require a balanced federal budget (like requirements in 49 states) with a 60 percent vote of both houses to opt out for emergencies. Line–item would give the president the same power many governors have, to strike selected items from a budget passed by the legislature, rather than be forced to veto the whole budget. Term limits and cutting spending rather than raising taxes are both self–explanatory.

Despite these popular opinions on these subjects, Congress has defeated the balanced budget amendment several times; has never considered the line–item veto; has had just one, three–hour hearing on term limits; and has repeatedly defeated the concept of cutting spending rather than raising taxes, most recently in defeating the Penny-Kasich spending reduction proposal. (On Penny-Kasich, see *What if Congress Were Term–Limited,* page 91.) Some congressional defeats of what the public emphatically wants would be reversed if long–term members of Congress were replaced by newer members, even of the same party.

Congressional Scandal

Any scandal that is obviously wrong to an average American, has continued over several years, is "suddenly" discovered, and comes as a total surprise to all involved.

This scene from *Casablanca* explains the special nature of congressional scandals:

> FRENCH CAPTAIN (in Rick's Cafe): I am shocked, shocked, to find gambling going on in this establishment.
>
> WAITER: Your winnings, sir. (Captain pockets his money.)

Information in the media made clear that the House Bank and the House Post Office not only were cesspools, but had been for years. Once stories broke, Speaker Foley claimed surprise; he promised to get to the bottom of things. That happened only after months of stone–walling in hopes the story would go away.

Similar linguistic distortion happens on critical subjects such as taxes and spending. Taxes become "contributions." Current spending becomes "investment." Any bill containing the words "reform" and "health care" is touted as actual reform of actual health care. Whether it really is, is wholly irrelevant. It only must seem that way. Increasingly, the public is catching on to these ploys.

In the last two years, such verbal distortion as the basis of political discourse has begun largely in the White House. But, Congress also being Democratic, its leaders have played along — either because they have no choice or because they do so willingly. Only occasionally has Congress allowed reality to intrude, and acted on the facts rather than perceptions of facts.

> ***Taxes as "Contributions"***
>
> Taxes and contributions will be the same thing when Girl Scouts get the authority to throw you in jail and take away your house, if you refuse to buy more cookies.

An example of Congress's attempting to cut through the administration's verbal fog in order to deal with the underlying reality, is its consideration of ending the arms embargo on the Bosnian Muslims. If the embargo ends, at least the Muslims will have a chance to defend themselves from the ongoing slaughter. As this is written, the outcome of that effort is unknown.

> ***Spending as "Investment"***
>
> Spending will be the same thing as investment when bankers get into poker games and bet their mortgage money to draw to an inside straight.

As this is written, the Clinton plan for health care seems as dead as a doornail, due to two points that are unacceptable to the public. One is higher taxes; the other is mandates on small businesses that will force many to stop hiring, lay off existing employees, or go out of business.

It also seems clear that some bill containing the words "health care" and "reform" will be passed by Congress before the next election. This Frankenstein legislation may be misshapen, cobbled together with body parts taken from the Clinton plan and others being bandied about in Congress. It will have bolts in its neck and will stumble as it walks. Still, the president will claim it as his own, and declare victory on the health care front.

> ***The Bosnia Option***
>
> When the choices are bad and the risks are high, above all else do not risk being a leader. Wait until the situation looks hopeless. Then take the lead in proposing more talks on a point certain to be rejected by others.
>
> ***The Health Care Shuffle***
>
> Demand health care reform; insist on impossible conditions. Claim credit for whatever passes, once the impossible conditions have been knocked out.

The same game is being played over violent crime. With grave differences between Senate and House versions of this bill, but an election looming, the least objectionable (least effective) parts of various plans will be slapped together. Congress and the president can say they "did something about crime."

The president has one method of getting out of the box of intractable and difficult problems. It is to hold a press conference and use words as a substitute for action, and theories as a substitute for plans.

Congress has a different method of dealing with the same situation. In Congress, nothing is final until it has gone to conference committee to iron out differences between House and Senate versions of any bill. Therefore, bold action can be proposed, and bold words spoken in support on the floor of either house, without any risk that bold action will result.

> ***The Crime Bill Twist***
>
> Come down hard on crime. Quietly insert provisions that will gut–shoot the death penalty, truth in sentencing, and reform in multiple appeals. Then claim victory over crime.
>
> ***The "Virtual Reality" Method***
>
> When a difficult problem arises, give a bang–up press conference. Promise to think about doing something. But don't actually do anything. (See "The Bosnia Option," "The Health Care Shuffle," and "The Crime Bill Twist.")

All government programs have a stated purpose. But few if any government programs have a checking process to find out whether they have fulfilled that purpose in the past, or are likely to do so in the future. The true purposes of government programs are something quite different. The super–conductor super–collider project, late of Texas, is a classic example.

> ***The Conference Committee Ploy***
>
> Pass whatever sounds good on the floor as long as congressional leaders are quietly on your side. Count on conference committees to chop out the best provisions and sneak back in the worst ones. (See, "The Crime Bill Twist" and "The Health Care Shuffle.")

Americans have now had more than a generation of watching expensive, sophisticated television commercials, designed to make viewers think that romance, health, youth, and happiness will be theirs if only they purchase the named product. As a result, we are a nation of competent cynics. We know from this experience how to distinguish between false claims and practical reality.

The people are able to weed through clever verbiage to discover the truth, if any, behind it. That translates readily into politics. Voters are not easily deceived, *if they have a choice.*

> ***The Super–Collider Definition***
>
> A government program is a success if it: (a) employs bureaucrats, (b) benefits special interests, (c) generates praise and campaign cash for Congress, and (d) the public has a dim idea what it is, or what it's supposed to accomplish.

Because of the vacillation of the White House on various subjects, domestic and foreign, that are important to the people, the normal advice to Democrats running for Congress in 1994 would be to keep their distance from President Clinton. After all, in special elections in Oklahoma and Kentucky this spring to fill vacant seats in Congress, Republicans soundly defeated Democrats by tying them to the White House.

This would be excellent advice, except incumbents need not pay attention to it. Both Democratic losses in special elections in 1994 occurred in open-seat races. For the reasons already described, House incumbents who are Democrats will be reelected regardless of attempts to tie them to the president.

> ***The Presidential Coattail Effect***
>
> Advice for Democratic candidates for Congress — recognize the president has no coattails, no coat, no shirt and no pants. He has either briefs or boxers. Hang onto those at your peril.

Different results will apply in the Senate, where races against incumbents are more even. One–term Democratic senators may be vulnerable; perhaps two–termers, but, not three–termers. For most of Congress it will be reelection as usual, with business as usual afterward.

Polls in Speaker Foley's district in February 1994 showed 47.0 percent of his voters want someone new. Only 43.0 percent thought he should be reelected. He will be comfortably reelected.

Similar polls in Dan Rostenkowski's district before his primary showed widespread dissatisfaction. But he won big, and will win bigger in the general. The problem is a lack of well–funded opposition. Neither the Illinois Republican Party nor major donors are giving his opponent significant support. They know Rosty will win and don't want the embarrassment of an all–out effort to unseat him that fails.

The Rostenkowski race is a microcosm of the entire House of Representatives. Incumbents win not because the voters prefer them, but because *there are no real choices.* No opponent, Democrat or Republican, could come close to matching Rosty's million–dollar campaign war chest.

4

Throw the Bums Out?

The Public's View of Term Limits

Polling on the subject of term limits for Congress has continued for more than 45 years. At the beginning, there was narrow support for limits, but no agreement on the length of term limits that should be established.

Today, however, the picture is much clearer. The support for term limits has risen to a two–thirds or more of the respondents. Also, the support now centers on two terms (12 years) for the Senate and three terms (six years) for the House.

In 1947, the Gallup Organization began asking the public in regular polls whether it favored or opposed term limits on senators (sometimes) or on all members of Congress, generally. For senators, the question was asked about two terms totaling 12 years. For members of the House, it was usually asked generally without specifying the number of terms or years, or in the early years was asked about a double subject. Increasing House terms to four years rather than two and combining that with three–term limits was the early, combined question.

With the exception of a single year, 1955, every time the question was asked in any form, the public answered with a resounding yes. (See Table H.) And the more years the question was asked, the higher became the margin of yes over no. At the same time, the public became more informed on term limits. The percentage of people responding "I don't know" dropped from a range of 7–13 percent in the early years to 3–4 percent in 1993.

The public view on term limits generally in 1947 supported them by 54 percent; opposed, 39 percent; and don't know, 7 percent. It has increased to 80 percent support, 17 percent opposition, and 3 percent undecided in 1993. The trend is massive. The public wants term limits.

The view of the people contrasts sharply with the views of congressmen, their staffs, and lobbyists who make their living seeking, and often getting, what they want for their clients by working with members and staff. (See Table I.)

Public Opinion on Term Limits, 1947–93

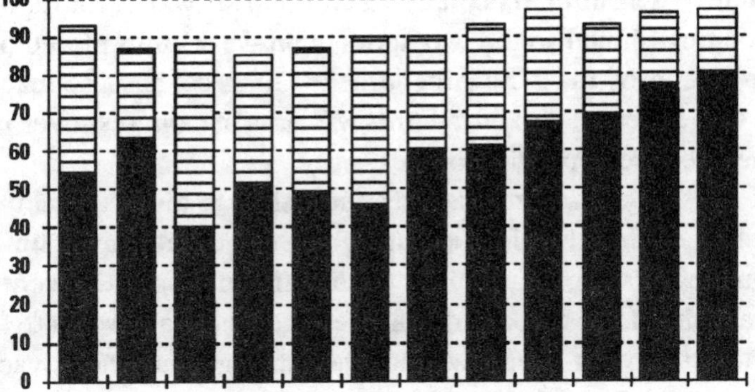

Opinion of Congressional Staff,
Bureaucrats and Lobbyists on Term Limits, 1992

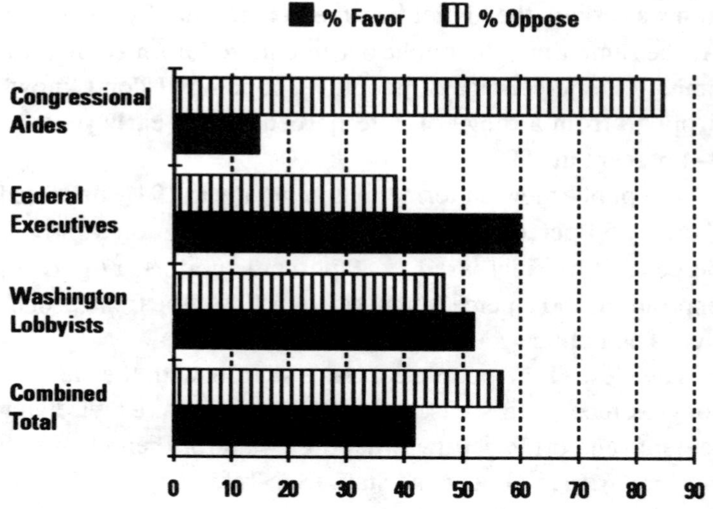

The difference between these two sets of numbers demonstrates as strongly as numbers on paper can, why the people believe that Congress is out of touch and no longer represents them. The public has made itself clear: it wants limits on Congress similar to the two–term, eight–year limits placed on presidents by the 22nd Amendment. Congress has also made itself perfectly clear; term limits will pass in Congress over its members dead political bodies.

Polls, of course, are theoretical snapshots in time of what the public apparently thinks about a given subject at a given time. Due to phrasing of questions or the effects of specific events, scandals, whatever, occurring at the time, polls can overstate or understate what people will do when they get into the privacy of the voting booths.

The ultimate "polls" are elections. Responses of "don't know" disappear, because people either vote for or against candidates and issues. There are no questions of sampling errors or how the question is phrased, because when the people vote they are actually making the decision posed for them.

Between 1990 and 1993, the citizens of 15 states and three of the nation's four largest cities had the opportunity to vote on term limits. These were not polls, but actual votes with actual results. Two votes took place in California: 1990, to limit terms of state officials; 1992, to limit congressmen; the later one is used. Two votes took place in Washington State; the later one is used. To avoid double counting, the vote in the city of Los Angeles is not included in the totals, since there was also a statewide vote in California.

These 15 states, plus New York City and Houston, represent 39.4 percent of the population of the United States. Since turnout is always much less than population, the 1992 vote for president in these jurisdictions is included for comparison.

Also, traditionally, total votes for any candidate or issue are less than the votes at the top of the ticket. Some voters just don't stay long enough to pull levers for referenda, which often appear at the bottom of the ballot. Still, these are massive vote totals. They confirm the polls about public opinion.

The Houston election was an anomaly. It was brought about by opponents of term limits. The Houston City Council, chafing under existing limits, put the proposal on the ballot to get rid of them. As the results show, the voters heartily disagreed.

All states shown were voting on term limits for Congress. In addition, California voted in limits for its state legislature in 1990, Proposition 140, 52–48 percent. Maine approved statewide limits in 1993, Question 5 won 67–33 percent. Oklahoma approved statewide limits in 1990, Question 632, also 67–33 percent. Colorado included statewide limits in the vote shown.

The last question about congressional term limits is not whether the public wants them, but how long they should be. There has always been general agreement that limits on the

Senate should be two terms, or 12 years total. There has not been, until recently, agreement on limitation on terms in the House. As the Gallup Organization polling indicates, three to five decades ago, the public debate assumed that limits on the House would provide them with the same number of years as the Senate, and therefore be either three terms of four years each, or six terms of two years each.

Other than the passionate desire of representatives to stay as long as possible, there is no logical reason why limits on the House should allow them as many years in office as the Senate. Plus, the original plan of the Congress at the Philadelphia Convention of 1787 was that the House would reflect the immediate concerns of the voters and the Senate would be more reserved and thoughtful. That difference, which has some logic behind it, would be better served by shorter limits on the House.

Votes for Term Limits in 15 States and 3 Cities, 1990–1993

State	**Year**	**Prop. #**	**Yes (millions)**	**% Yes**	**No (millions)**	**% No**
Ariz.	92	Prop. 107	1.02	74	0.36	26
Ark.	92	Amend. 4	0.49	60	0.33	40
Calif.	92	Prop. 165	6.58	63	3.77	37
Colo.	90	Amend. 5	0.65	71	0.27	29
Fla.	92	Amend. 9	3.63	77	1.10	23
Mich.	92	Prop. B	2.32	59	1.63	41
Mo.	92	Amend. 12	1.59	74	0.56	26
Mont.	92	Init. 64	0.26	67	0.13	33
Neb.	92	Meas. 407	0.48	68	0.22	32
N.D.	92	Meas. 5	0.16	55	0.13	45
Ohio	92	Amend. 2	2.90	66	1.48	34
Ore.	92	Meas. 3	1.00	69	0.44	31
S.D.	92	Amend. A	0.21	63	0.12	37
Wash.	92	Init. 573	1.12	52	1.02	48
Wyo.	92	Init. 2	0.15	77	0.04	23
Cities	**Year**	**Prop. #**				
Hou.	91	Prop. 2	0.15	57	0.11	43
LA	93	Amend. 2	0.27	65	0.14	35
NY	93	Prop. 4	0.58	60	0.39	40
Totals:	(minus LA)		23.29	67	11.60	33

Clinton, 43.7, 43%; Bush, 38.1, 38%; Perot, 19.2; 19%

As discussed in Chapter 6, a six–term limit for the House will establish three "safe" elections and three competitive elections for House members seeking to remain in office for the whole 12 years. A three–term limit would create three competitive elections, increasing the opportunity for the voters to express clearly their current views on public issues through the election of new representatives in Congress.

This is not merely speculation. The study of 50 years of elections of governors, comparing those in states with limits to those in states without limits, proves that *limits create competition even in elections in which an incumbent is free to run one more time.* (See *Governors Elections,* page 72.)

The public's views now correspond to the real–world experience shown in that study. Almost a clear majority want three–term limits, with a two–term limit as the second most acceptable choice. So, the proposal now kicking around the House of capitulating, when pushed hard enough, on six terms (meaning 12 years) is yet another example that Congress just doesn't get it.

Even more important than the overall results are the demographic breakdowns of the results. New York City is especially instructive. Republicans constituted only 18 percent of the voters at the polls. Limits could prevail in New York City only with Democratic votes and with black votes. And limits got support from both groups.

Many opponents of term limits charge that they are a "white, Republican, conservative" plot to oust from office Democrats who cannot be defeated in straight–up elections. The last time anyone checked, white, Republican, conservative voters in New York City could hold a convention in a large phone booth. Almost all the officeholders in New York who will be affected by limits are Democrats, many of them of color, who will surely be replaced by other Democrats of color.

The bottom line in this election was the same as in the song "New York, New York," as sung by Old Blue–Eyes himself: "If I can make it there, I'll make it anywhere...." There is zero question that the public supports term limits in all large jurisdictions, beginning with Congress and working down to large states, large cities, and large counties. The fall elections in 1994 will provide additional evidence of this fact. But the results in 1992 and 1993 already prove it.

Unless the public has changed its mind, the 1994 results will be the same. And there is no reason to think the public has changed its view on limits.

At the state and local levels, limits are usually two terms of four years each, since there are few two–year terms left in state and local government. Some jurisdictions have chosen the method of two terms then sit out a term, rather than a lifetime ban after anyone has served in a specific office for two terms.

There is no great difference between these two choices. The power of incumbency dissipates after an incumbent has left office for a term. The person elected meanwhile has gained the power of incumbency. Therefore, sitting out a term has about the same effect in avoiding the evils of long–time officeholders as a lifetime ban after two terms.

The disrespect the public feels for Congress specifically, and for long–term incumbents in offices at all levels, will play itself out in the elections of 1994 not in the defeat of incumbents, but in the passage of term limits.

The Sleeping Dog Caveat

Miguel Cervantes warned, almost four centuries ago in *Don Quixote,* "Let sleeping dogs lie." Congress has ignored that warning. Decades of abuse awoke the sleeping dog of public opinion. It will not sleep again until Congress pays the price — with term limits.

Exit Poll on Term Limits, New York City, 1993

(Opposition is 100 percent minus support; "don't know" responses are eliminated. Majorities in favor are in boldface.)

Democrat, **55%**; Republican, **76%**; independent and other, **59%**

Income (in 1,000s): less than $15, **60%**; $15–$30, **64%**; $30–50, **62%**; $50–$75, **57%**; $75–100, **68%**; $100+, 48%

Education: high school grad., **69%**; some college, **64%**; college grad., **57%**; post grad., 47%

Ideology: Conservative, **68%**; Moderate, **64%**; Liberal, 48%

Religion: Protestant, **58%**; Catholic, **71%**, Other Christian, **63%**; Jewish, 45%; Other, **55%**; None, 45%

Union Member: yes, **59%**; no, **58%**

First–Time Voter: yes, **59%**; no, **59%**

Employment: employed, **59%**; unemployed & looking, **60%**

New York City is: more safe, 49%; less safe, **67%**; same, **51%**

Ethnic Background: Italian, **80%**; Irish, **59%**; African, **53%**; Eastern European, **53%**; Puerto Rican, **68%**; Other, 49%

5

"Rotation in Office"

The Views of the Framers

The philosophy of term limits should be compared with American political theory, especially with the views of those who shaped the American Constitution. But, the roots of what the people are now doing with term limits go deeper into American soil than merely the Constitutional Convention in 1787.

The first American political document, the first "constitution," was written in 1620. The Mayflower Compact has only 70 operative words, yet they express the central ideas of all American political theory. Government, its officials, and its laws are created by the people, and the people have the right and the power to change them whenever they deem appropriate.

> In the name of God Amen. We whose names are underwritten, the loyall subjects of our dread soveraigne Lord King James.... Haveing undertaken... a voyage to plant the first colonie in the Northerne parts of Virginia...

> ...covenant & combine our selves together into a civill body politck; for better ordering & preservations & furtherance of the ends aforesaid; and by virtue hearof to enacte, constitute, and frame shuch just & equall lawes, ordinances, Acts, constitutions, & offices, from time to time, as shall be thought most meete & convenient for the generall good of the Colonie; unto which we promise all due submission and obedience.

Of the 102 passengers aboard the *Mayflower* who survived to reach Plymouth Rock on Cape Cod, November 11, 1620, 41 signed this document: heads of families, bachelors, and most of the man servants. (The idea of political rights for women was entirely foreign to this body.)

The important parts are two: the people established their own government, and by the phrase "from time to time" they reserved the right to change what they had done, as the need for change became apparent.

Perhaps the most elegant statement of these concepts, a statement only now winning favor with more than half of the world's governments, is in the Declaration of Independence, written by Thomas Jefferson, promulgated on July 4, 1776.

> We hold these truths to be self–evident, that all men are created equal, that they are endowed by their Creator with certain unalienable Rights, that among these are Life, Liberty and the pursuit of Happiness —
>
> That to secure these rights, Governments are instituted among Men, deriving their just powers from the consent of the governed, — That whenever any Form of Government becomes destructive of these ends, it is the Right of the People to

> alter or abolish it, and to institute new Government, laying its foundation on such principles and organizing its powers in such form, as to them shall seem most likely to effect their Safety and Happiness.

The first attempt to create a national government to carry out these principles was the Articles of Confederation. With the abuses from King George III fresh in their minds, the Congress and the States feared the establishment of a new tyranny on American shores. Therefore, they created under the Articles a government too weak to function competently.

By 1785 the government of the United States was bankrupt. Its diplomats in Europe functioned primarily as beggars for high–interest loans from other nations. It was too weak politically to enforce the peace treaty it had won from England on the battlefield. Shays' Rebellion broke out in Massachusetts, because an unpaid veteran of the Revolutionary War, Daniel Shays, lost his farm for nonpayment of a $12 property tax bill. It seemed the United States would fragment into disconnected and perhaps warring pieces.

In that context, the Framers met in Philadelphia in 1787 to create a new form of government and to write a Constitution to maintain it for future generations.

Patrick Henry was chosen to be a delegate from Virginia. He refused to go, reportedly saying, "I smelt a rat." He was a leader of the Anti–Federalists in Virginia, and eloquently urged the ratifying Convention there to reject the proposed Constitution.

> ***Patrick Henry, Nonattending Delegate from Virginia***
>
> "The only semblance of a check [on Congress] is the negative power of not reelecting them. This sir, is a feeble barrier, when their personal interest, their ambition and avarice, come to be put in contrast with the happiness of the people."

Most of the Framers of the Constitution — authors of the political system we still use today — wrote in favor of "rotation in office," which is the original phrase for what term limits seek to accomplish today. They had reason for that belief.

Term limits had existed under the Articles of Confederation. They were left out of the Constitution, which leads some commentators today to assume the Framers did not intend regular change in the elected officeholders. That assumption is false.

> ***Pennsylvania Constitution of 1776***
>
> "[T]he danger of establishing an inconvenient aristocracy [will] be effectively prevented." This was stated in justifying a limit of no more than four one–year terms in seven years for its state legislators.

Jefferson, who was Ambassador to France during the Constitutional Convention, made this comment in a letter to James Madison after he received a copy of the proposed Constitution. He was not referring to the concept of rotation in office, which he strongly supported. He was referring to the omission of mandatory term limits in the Constitution.

> ***Thomas Jefferson, Non–delegate***
>
> "[Another] feature I dislike, and strongly dislike, is the abandonment in every instance of the principle of rotation in office...."

Most of the Framers used contemporary experience as their guide and assumed rotation would continue to happen naturally and mandatory limits were unnecessary. Jefferson was more far–sighted. He may have been the most prescient political scientist the United States has ever produced. As President Kennedy remarked at his first dinner for Nobel Laureates, "There has never been such an assemblage of intellect in the White House since Thomas Jefferson dined here, alone."

Although Jefferson was not a delegate, he had a role in the framing of the Constitution. Before leaving for Paris he assembled from his own library a collection of books on history and politics for his friend James Madison. At the time, Jefferson had the most extensive library in the United States. His source materials and his conversations with Madison contributed to the Virginia Plan, which Madison and Governor Edmund Randolph presented to the Convention. The Plan, which did contain term limits, became the framework of both the debates and the Constitution itself.

So, though Jefferson cannot correctly be called a Framer, his service to the United States was much broader than that. He, more than any other individual, was the creator of American political theory as expressed in the Declaration of Independence, the Constitution, and the Bill of Rights.

The Supreme Court has recognized his towering contribution in major cases on freedom of the press and freedom of religion. If only one voice should be heeded from the period when the Constitution was framed, it should be the man who was in Paris, Thomas Jefferson. No one else from that period better understood the structural reasons for term limitations to preserve the then–unique kind of government that was born in Philadelphia in 1787.

At Philadelphia, term limits were extensively discussed concerning the presidency. Alexander Hamilton represented the extreme, autocratic view. He believed the president should be elected for life, and should have an absolute veto (not a veto that could be overridden) on the acts of Congress. The discussion was renewed several times, with consideration of a single term of four, five, six or seven years for the president. Finally, the Convention settled on a four–year term, without answering the question of reelection.

> ***George Mason, Virginia Delegate***
>
> "[Representatives] ought to mix with the people, think as they think, feel as they feel — ought to be perfectly amenable to them, and thoroughly acquainted with their interest and condition."

The delegates understood that George Washington would almost certainly be elected first president of the United States under its new government. Washington privately expressed a disapproval of limiting the election of the president, so the idea of term limits for that office was dropped. However, by his actions, Washington demonstrated his belief that elected officials should not remain long in public office. Near the end of his second term as president he announced he would not run again. He retired to Mount Vernon to live out his days under the authority of the nation whose destinies he had guided.

Term limits for Congress were barely considered at the Constitutional Convention. Senators were to be chosen by the members of the state legislatures. Senators were answerable to the legislatures in the performance of their duties. For 124 years, state legislatures would "instruct" their senators how to vote on subjects of strong interest. And senators would vote accordingly, since the same legislatures that selected them had the power to replace them. This control over senators was broken in 1913, when the 17th Amendment was adopted, making senators popularly elected, rather than chosen by the state legislatures.

Concerning the House, the experience of Congress under the Articles of Confederation was instructive. Though the Articles provided for representatives to leave office periodically, the states controlled the election laws under which they were selected. There was no enforcement mechanism (under the Articles there was no Supreme Court, nor any tradition that a ruling by such a court was binding). When a few representatives were elected beyond the requirements, Congress did nothing to enforce the Articles.

Alexander Hamilton, New York Delegate

"[Representatives] should have an immediate dependence on, and immediate sympathy with, the people."

Besides, the experience of the Framers was that elected officials voluntarily left office after one or two terms. They went home to live under the laws they had written. Others took their places as new representatives.

The perceived problem then was that democracy might be too active. As Alexander Hamilton wrote in *The Federalist,* No. 78, the government should not be altered "whenever a momentary inclination happens to lay hold of a majority." The Senate and president were indirectly elected, to be restraints on too much democracy as reflected in House elections.

> ***Charles Pinckney, South Carolina Delegate***
>
> "A longer term would fix them at the seat of government. They would acquire an interest there, perhaps transfer their property, and lose sight of the states they represent." He was arguing for four-year terms for the Senate.

Consider one objection raised against the Constitution by the Anti–Federalists, the main opponents to its adoption in Philadelphia and to its ratification by the states. The Anti–Federalists asserted that the two–year terms for the House were too long, that the representatives would therefore be too removed from the current will of the people. They cited the slogan "Where annual elections end, tyranny begins." Then there was the example of the most democratic state, Rhode Island, referred to as Rogue Island. (It had new elections for its legislature every six months.) Rhode Island refused to send delegates to the Philadelphia Convention. For four years it refused to ratify the Constitution and rejoin the Union. It even conducted the only referendum on the Constitution, and ratification lost by a wide margin. Ultimately, economic and political pressures caused Rhode Island to ratify, and rejoin the United States.

Despite the example of democracy run amok in Rhode Island, the Framers favored frequent elections and thought they would also mean high turnover in the representatives chosen. This assumption was correct for 125 years. Today it is false. That change goes to the heart of the drive for term limits.

Also, as discussed above in the difference between shoe–leather districts and media ones, the representatives then ran in districts of only 30,000 people. It was both easy and inexpensive for new candidates, perhaps expressing new and different ideas, to win election to the House.

In short, term limits were left out of the Constitution as written not because the Framers had ceased to believe in rotation in office, but because they were satisfied that rotation would occur even without any constitutional compulsions.

> ***Roger Sherman,***
> ***Connecticut Delegate***
>
> "The more permanency [government] has, the worse, if it be a bad government. Frequent elections are necessary to preserve the good behavior of rulers."
>
> ***John Adams,***
> ***Massachusetts Delegate***
>
> "These great men... should be elected once a year — like bubbles on the sea of matter borne, they rise, they break, and to that sea return."

Recall the quotation from *Cato's Letters* which appears in Chapter 3. The tendency of long–term officials to "grow in conceit," and become "a different species from their fellow subjects," is an unfortunate but common product of human nature. As Lord Acton wrote, "Power corrupts, and absolute power corrupts absolutely."

> ***George Mason,***
> ***Virginia Delegate***
>
> "Nothing is so essential to a republican government as a periodical rotation. Nothing so strongly impels a man to regard the interest of his constituents as the certainty of returning to the general mass of the people, from whence he was taken...."

The US Constitution is the oldest surviving constitution in the world in part because it accommodates both the best and worst of human nature. It allows change and accomplishment, but it creates multiple barriers, not just the familiar checks and balances but also the federal structure itself, against the tendency to corruption and failure.

After his presidency, Thomas Jefferson began a long correspondence with John Adams, once his archenemy politically. By the end of their lives, these two giants of American history were close friends. They died within hours of each other on July 4, 1826, the 50th anniversary of the Declaration of Independence. During their correspondence, Jefferson wrote this statement that describes broadly the need for constitutional restraints on government, and narrowly the need for term limits:

> In every government on earth is some trace of human weakness, some germ of corruption and degeneracy, which cunning will discover, wickedness insensibly open, cultivate and improve. Every government degenerates when trusted to the rulers of the people alone. The people themselves therefore are its only safe repository.

The battle for ratification of the Constitution was fierce, and its outcome was very much in doubt until New York (whose absence would have split the Union in two) and Virginia (the largest state, with one–sixth of the population) narrowly ratified within days of each other. James Madison wrote the Virginia Plan, which grew into the Constitution. He also wrote, along with Alexander Hamilton and John Jay, the series of newspaper articles in New York called *The Federalist.*

This book justified, item by item and clause by clause, all the provisions of the Constitution. On only one point was *The Federalist* clearly incorrect; the need for a Bill of Rights. The opponents of the Constitution demanded it, and the Framers finally conceded one would be added. That concession brought about ratification in New York, Virginia and Massachusetts.

In 1790 James Madison, now a Virginia Congressman, drafted the 12 amendments proposed as the Bill of Rights.

In *The Federalist,* No. 51, Madison paralleled Jefferson's thinking on the nature of government, and the need for constitutional restraints on government officials. He wrote:

> [W]hat is government itself but the greatest of all reflections on human nature? If men were angels,

> no government would be necessary. If angels were to govern men,.. [no] controls on government would be necessary. In framing a government... [by] men over men, the great difficulty lies in this: you must first enable the government to control the governed; and in the next place oblige it to control itself.

Many of the quotations in this chapter come from an excellent article in the *Hofstra Law Review,* "Will the Gentlemen Please Yield? A Defense of the Constitutionality of State-Imposed Term Limitations." Those interested in exploring the Framers' views will find the article cited in the Bibliography.

The term limits effort today is nothing more, or less, than an effort by the people to reestablish control over their government, which they have lost by degrees to professional politicians who believe that government is too important to be left to the people. The supreme arrogance of the Foley Forces is their assault on the central premise of American political theory, that the people possess the ultimate sovereign power.

The words that Abraham Lincoln spoke on the battlefield of Gettysburg on November 19, 1863, apply to the bloodless war now being fought over term limits:

> Four score and seven years ago our fathers brought forth on this continent, a new nation, conceived in liberty, and dedicated to the proposition that all men are created equal....
>
> ...we here highly resolve....that this nation, under God, shall have a new birth of freedom — and that government of the people, by the people, for the people, shall not perish from the earth.

What we have acquired in the era of Speakers Tip O'Neill, Jim Wright, and now Tom Foley, is government of the government, by the government and for the government. Only "rotation in office," brought about by term limits, can change that corrupt and closed system.

Bloodless wars, of course, are neither as dramatic nor as terminal as was the Civil War. The United States will not cease to exist if term limits somehow fail. However, without limits, the rights and powers of the people, the respect for government, the health of the nation's economy, and most important, the freedoms of the people, will continue their steady erosion. The stakes are subtle, but nonetheless overwhelming.

Alexander Hamilton said this, in justifying the establishment of the Electoral College, in *The Federalist,* No. 68: "Talents for low intrigue and the little arts of popularity may alone suffice to elevate a man to first honors [governorship] in a single state, but it will require other talents, and a different kind of merit, to establish him in the esteem and confidence of the whole union... [to become] President of the United States."

Might it be true that "talents for low intrigue and the little arts of popularity" have come to dominate the membership of Congress, especially in the House? Opponents of term limits have argued that term limits might bring in a new crop of officeholders who would be worse. But, the public has already answered that charge. With Congress holding only a 19 percent approval rating, there is little room for it to get worse.

The philosophical underpinnings of term limits have been explored in much greater depth by other writers, and need not be repeated here. Those interested in pursuing the subject in depth could read George Will's excellent 1992 book, *Restoration: Congress, Term Limits, and the Recovery of Deliberative Democracy.*

Term limits are the way to restore what the Framers both expected and practiced — rotation into office of new representatives, bringing to the nation's capitol, state capitols, and major cities, fresh commitment and a closer attachment to the views of the people back home.

6

Half a Million Officeholders

Term Limits at the State and Local Levels

If a government means an entity having elected leaders and possessing the power to tax and to condemn property, then there are more than 80,000 governments in the United States today. Half of these are special purpose governments, most of them school boards, plus others such as sewer districts, water districts in the West, and other special purpose entities as decided locally.

The other 40,000 are the state governments, plus elected governments in all but the most sparsely populated counties, plus cities, towns, and townships. These are all "general" governments. Within the limits of their charters (the constitutions of local government), they have the power to pass all laws and do all acts which the people deem appropriate, as reflected through their elected representatives.

No exact count of all these governments and their elected officials exists, but there are about 500,000 elected officials in these governments. There are 7,400 state legislators, allowing for some vacancies. All the rest are local officials.

In one area of state and local government the experience with term limits is long, and clear. Governors of some states, and before them "presidents" of some colonies, have been term–limited. Because modern elections are radically different from elections in the 18th and 19th centuries, much of this experience with term–limited governors can be ignored as irrelevant to modern times. However, from 1940 to 1990, 28 states had one of three kinds of term limits for their governors.

This 50–year period was selected because mass media existed in this time span. Radio was in widespread use at the beginning, TV at the end. The size of states had grown to the point that the "district" size for governors was similar to the districts for the House of Representatives. (It was not until 1921 that Congress fixed the size of the House permanently at 435 members, meaning that with each new census, districts would grow, instead of the House adding new members.)

The direct experience with the results of term limits in some states compared to the lack of limits in others has been known for decades. For whatever reason, the political scientists and other "experts" who pontificate on the merits or demerits of term limits never studied this comparative experiment in the real world. The first such study of this comparison was made by this author in 1991.

Fifty Years of Governors Elections:
Comparison of Limited and Nonlimited Elections

There were 802 gubernatorial elections in this 50 years. Of these, 411 took place in term–limited states; 164 of them were specifically term–limited elections. The rest were nonlimited elections. The usual pattern for limits was a requirement that governors sit out a term after serving two consecutive terms. Four states allowed no consecutive terms, meaning every election was term–limited. Two states had lifetime limits, serve two terms then never run again.

The 28 states that had term limits for governor in 1940—90 range from large to small and are located in all parts of the country. The same applies to the 22 states that had no limits for governor. There is no reason to believe that the voters in the first group of states are any more likely, or less likely, to want changes in their governors than those in the second group. But the results from the two are radically different.

The study measured political change by party changes among governors and by comparing party elections for governor with the party majorities elected in the two houses of the state legislatures. (Nebraska's unicameral senate was not included since its members were elected on a nonpartisan basis.)

The study assumed that in smaller districts voters are more likely to elect officials who reflect their current views, unaffected by large amounts of money provided by special interests. At the low end of the scale was the New Hampshire house in 1990; with only 2,117 citizens per legislator, these are definitely shoe–leather districts. The opposite end of the scale is the California Senate, with 772,000 citizens per district. These are even larger media districts than those for US representatives.

In general, the state senates are two or three times smaller than the state houses, except New Hampshire where the ratio is 16.7 to 1.0. The smallest state senate is 40 members (California). Senators, and house members to an even greater degree, are elected from smaller districts than governors. Therefore, the legislative elections should be a better barometer of current views of the public than the gubernatorial ones.

The study asked two questions: Was the party of the governor *more* likely to change in term–limited elections than non–limited ones? Was divided government, meaning the party of the governor is different from the party of the houses of the legislature, less likely to occur in term–limited elections than nonlimited ones?

It is not surprising that the answer to these two questions was yes. It may be surprising how powerful the results were.

In garden variety political polling by CBS, the *New York Times, Newsweek* and the like, the "margin of error" reported in the fine print at the bottom is usually 3.5 percent. That means a 95 percent probability that the real answer, if the whole population was polled, would be within 3.5 percent up or down from the result stated. For instance, if the poll says Smith has a lead over Jones of 51 to 49 percent, it is a statistical tie.

The key is 95 percent probability. That is considered acceptable in social science research. The results on term limits for governors were much higher. It was one hundred times more likely (99.95 percent) that the increased party changes for governor were due to the presence of term limits in those elections. A total of 56 elections in the nonlimited states would have gone the other way, if those states had had term limits in effect.

The same happened on divided government. It was ten times more likely (99.5 percent) that divided government would result in nonlimited elections than in term–limited ones. A total of 29 elections would have come out differently if all states had had term limits.

The final comparison is more subtle, and extremely important. *All* gubernatorial elections in term–limited states were compared with all elections in nonlimited states. On the face of it, term limits should have no effect whatever on an election where the incumbent is free to run and win one more time. But appearances can be deceiving.

It was ten times more likely than standard research (99.5 percent) that divided government would not result in *all* elections in term–limited states, than in nonlimited ones. This meant that governors who were incumbents, *who were free to run again,* were still being defeated for reelection much more often in states with term limits than in those without limits.

Why should limits affect the election chances of an incumbent who is not yet limited? The answer goes a long way toward explaining why members of the House of Representatives are the most durable form of incumbents in the universe today.

There is a huge difference between "sacrificial lamb" opposition candidates and genuine opposition candidates. The sacrificial lambs are often nominees of a party that expects to lose, but wants a decent candidate running so he/she will not cause losses all down the ticket, including races the opposition party might otherwise win. More often, the lambs are self–sacrificing. Candidates with lesser qualifications, smaller and less able staff, and, most important, far less fundraising capacity, enter the race for governor hoping lightning will strike and they will win.

Genuine candidates, on the other hand, make their decision to run a year or more in advance. They put together experienced and able campaign staffs. They put together able finance committees that can and do raise the kind of money necessary for a competent campaign in their state. And they can do those things because the candidates themselves have more experience and better qualifications.

Now, consider the common term–limited situation where Governor Curley was elected last time, can run again, and is running again. If Curley wins this time, he will be barred from the next election. It will become an open–seat race. The long–term logic of an opposite party candidate is to lock up the nomination of his/her party *next* time when chances of success are best.

But the way to own the *next* nomination is to run a solid, well–financed campaign *this* time and do very well, even if in a losing cause.

Consider the kind of events that happen in the real world and affect elections. Governors die or become disabled; they get indicted or involved in scandals; or they suddenly find themselves on the wrong side of an issue about which the public cares deeply. Any or all of these things can happen at any time. In a four–year term, they will happen in the last year, within 12 months of the next election, one–quarter of the time.

When opportunity knocks, who will be there to answer the door? In nonlimited states, the opposition party candidate will more often be a sacrificial lamb. Governor Curley gets wounded, but the opponent isn't strong enough to take advantage and win the election.

It is quite different in term–limited states. The opposition candidate already in the field is more likely to be strong with a strong campaign, ready and able to take advantage of such unexpected opportunities. So, Curley gets defeated.

In short, incumbent governors in term–limited states get defeated more often in the election *before* the one when they'll be limited because the caliber of their opposition is better. And the caliber is better because of the prospects of term limits one election down the road.

This analysis of gubernatorial elections is very important in considering the kind of limits that should be placed on US representatives. House members are elected for only two years. Random distribution of crippling political disasters means they will occur 50 percent of the time during the 12 months preceding the election. But since a solid opposition candidate needs a 12–month lead time to decide to run, organize and raise money, it means members of the House are the kind of incumbent least likely to face solid challengers, most likely to be up against sacrificial lambs.

Some people, many of them representatives who are thinking narrowly of their own futures, are suggesting that the House limit should be six terms (12 years) to match the two–term (12–year) limit generally agreed for senators. Most leaders of term limits across the country prefer three terms (six years) as the House limit.

The whole point of term limits is to make elections more competitive, so the will of the people is more likely to be expressed rather than stifled. From the standpoint of creating competitive elections, the choice between six terms and three is critical. If representatives serve no more than three terms, the first election will be competitive by definition because that's the one where the representative came in as a freshman. The third election will also be competitive, because that's the one where an opposition candidate will be positioning himself to own the nomination for the open–seat election to come.

If the pattern is three terms, only the second election will be noncompetitive, since potential opponents won't want to run and lose twice before the seat becomes open. However, historically the first reelection campaign for a representative is more competitive than any of the dozens that may follow. So, even that middle election will be somewhat competitive.

The situation changes sharply if the House limit is six terms. The first and last (sixth) elections will be competitive, just as before. The second will be somewhat competitive, just as before. But in the middle elections, the third, fourth and fifth, the incumbents will have the same type of free ride as Speaker Foley, or Congressmen McDade and Rostenkowski.

Three terms for the House will mean more than two–thirds of all House elections will become competitive. Once the predictions in this book of the House races this fall prove out, the results will demonstrate that less than one–twentieth of all House elections are presently competitive.

On the other hand, if the House gets a six–term limit, more than half of all its elections will be the same–old, same–old. Most incumbents, just not as many as now, will cruise to reelection regardless of merit, political views, or anything other than massive fundraising ability.

The logic of the race before the open seat for governors applies, but in a different way, to senators. If senators serve at most two terms, their freshman election will obviously be competitive. Their second election will also be competitive because the most likely opponent from the opposite party will be either a governor who can run without leaving office, or a candidate who is positioning himself to run either for governor in four years, or the other senate seat in two or four years.

Either way, term limits will make *all* Senate elections competitive. Today it is the calendar and the actuarial tables, not the competition, that most threaten senators who have already won two elections.

In state–level elections, the problem of entrenched incumbents has not seemed as acute as in Congress. However, that may be due to a lack of looking for it. *Michigan Commentary* in June 1993 ran an article by Public Sector Consultants, Inc., that analyzed potential effects of limits on terms of state legislators voted in there in 1992. The article included these eye–popping statistics:

> Job security — despite the need to face election every two or four years — was much better than in much of the private sector. Since 1961 the chances of an incumbent state senator or representative losing an election were about equal to the chances of dying while in office: one in 50. Since 1967, in 2,860 general and primary elections for the House, only 63 incumbents lost, and in 456 primary or general elections for the Senate during the same period, only 18 incumbents were defeated. Serving in the legislature has been good steady work, where a breadwinner could support a family and plan for a comfortable retirement — a secure and rewarding career for those who chose to stay.

In short, more and more, the same problem of untouchable incumbents is spreading down through the ranks of state legislators as exists at the federal level. Because the districts are smaller and there has been relatively high turnover in most state legislatures until recent years, the perceived need for term limits at this level is new. One of the first states to establish them was California in 1990, through passage of Proposition 140.

The 1992 California Legislature: Predicting the Results for a Term–Limited Congress?

After Proposition 140 was challenged unsuccessfully all the way to the US Supreme Court by Speaker Willie Brown and his cohorts, it was clear in early 1992 term limits were coming, and nothing could stop them. Although limits will not force any members of the California Assembly or Senate from office prior to 1996, an unexpected change occurred in 1992. Before, during and even after the election, one–quarter of the members of that legislature, 30 of the 120 members of the assembly and senate, resigned to take full–time jobs in the private sector, in education or in government.

Neither term limit supporters nor opponents had anticipated this reaction. Yet, in context of California politics it made sense. More members of that legislature than of any other in the nation, listed their occupations as "full–time legislator." California had more instances than any other state of seats of legislators who retired, were elected to higher office, or went to prison, being passed down to their administrative aides. There was even one instance of a three–generation "hereditary" seat: the aide/member passing it on to the next aide/member, to the next aide/member.

In short, most members of the California legislature looked on it as a permanent, lifetime position, with a fat pension at the end. (Another, little–noticed part of Proposition 140 cut out the fat pensions.)

The common denominators of the jobs taken by the sudden retirees from the legislature are two. First, they pay well and seem secure. Second, they have something to do with public policy, lobbying, or communicating with the state of California. In short, they got new jobs promptly, before limits fully kicked in to make used legislators a drug on the market for employment.

In California, limits had a "foreshadowing" effect. The kind of officeholders that term limits are intended to force out, leave early once term limits are established. What kind of legislators are taking their place?

One charge of opponents of term limits is that they are a thinly veiled plot by conservatives and Republicans to knock Democrats and liberals out of office. That was not the result in California. Republicans lost one seat, essentially a draw. However, women, minorities, people from the private sector, older candidates than present members were when they were elected, were winners in the open–seat elections in California in 1992. Of course, long–term veterans won almost all the seats they cared to run for again.

Freshman legislators elected in 1992 were 33.8 percent of the California Assembly, a larger class than any other since 1946. And the changes were not just in new faces.

Prior to the 1992 election, the California legislature invited Mark Russell to address it at a private dinner. In his comments he said, "I've been on a tour of state legislatures.... Mostly they are a bunch of fat white guys pretending to hurt one another." Humor, of course, only works when based on a kernel of truth, as this was.

Women in the California legislature, both houses, jumped from 22 to 29 in the 1992 election, an increase of one–third. Whites, who were only 57 percent of the population in the 1990 census, held onto 80 percent of the 120 total seats. Latinos, who are a quarter of the state's population, had 8.3

percent of all seats. Asian–Americans gained their first state senator. African–Americans, who are 7 percent of the population, gained 7.5 percent of the seats.

The gains for women and minorities are important, but so are the changes in the attitudes and work product of the legislature. For the first time in seven years, the California legislature passed the budget on time. Then, the new legislators engineered a solution to the Workmen's Compensation law that had been in trouble and unsolvable by the former legislature.

A statement from Assemblywoman Valerie Brown of Sonoma on her first day in office accurately described the new breed of legislators in Sacramento:

> We tend to be older, we come from business backgrounds, not government.... [T]here is going to be a reluctance to buy into the rituals and expectations. There isn't time to do the dancing. That doesn't mean I don't respect the system, but it will be my charge to make the system work for me and the people I represent.

Assemblywoman Brown, well educated, owner of a small business, and a Democrat, is a harbinger of what incumbent-encrusted state legislatures and large city and county governments across the country can expect after the elections of 1994. Term limits will bring to public office at all levels thousands of new people like her. And the public welcomes that prospect.

What happened in California also applies to the Congress of the United States.

In 1992, the 40 California Senate districts had grown to an average size of 772,000, much more than the 585,000 in the average US House district. California Assembly districts had grown to 386,000 on average, comparable to House districts.

There were also strong parallels in fundraising and campaign spending. The average costs of winning campaigns in 1992 for the California Senate, US House, and California Assembly were $628,000, $528,000, and $434,000 — in proportion to district size as expected under analyses previously made.

In California as in Congress, the bulk of the money came from organizations doing business with the government. In California as in Congress, special interests favored incumbents over challengers and open–seat candidates, though the margins in California were far less lopsided.

Recall the discussion in Chapter 2 about "leadership PACs" in Congress attracting major donations. The Speaker of the California Assembly, Willie Brown, raised over $2,200,000. His own election contest, his 19th, was a walk–over. He saved the money, either to reward his friends and punish his enemies, or to position himself to obtain a seat in the California Senate when his assembly days are over, or both.

The need for money to run in "media districts" is even greater in the California legislative races than in Congress on average. Many of the nation's largest (and most expensive) media markets are in California, including of course the largest one of all, Los Angeles.

Where does the money to run come from? The *California Political Almanac* for 1993–94 refers to certain committees of the California legislature as "juice" committees, ones which regulate large and prosperous interests with a history of generosity to committee members' campaign war chests. And who names every chairman and co–chairman of the assembly committees? Speaker Brown does. Now his $2,200,000 war chest for a state assemblyman makes excellent sense.

If die–hard opponents of term limits in the Congress want to see their future, they need look no further than the crystal ball of the California legislative elections of 1992. As Alan Rosenthal of Rutgers University said, "[T]he nearest thing to Congress outside of Washington, D.C. [is] California. [It] is way out there beyond where any other legislatures are in terms of political partisanship, full–time campaigning, and the cost of campaigns. California is almost another nation."

At the other end of the political scale from California are the local jurisdictions across the United States where term limits are being raised as an issue in 1994. Limits are much more recent in their application to most local elections, in cities, counties, townships, and the like.

There are hundreds of local jurisdictions which have already established term limits for their elected officials in their charters. There are tens of thousands, especially the smallest cities, towns and counties, where term limits are totally unnecessary. But local governments which have limits are still a small fraction of those in which limits would increase the responsiveness of local officials to their constituents.

US Term Limits, the leading organization for limits on officials at all levels, has begun in 1994 a project called Term Limits Everywhere! Though this effort is in its nascent stages, as of June 1, 1994, it seemed likely that term limits would appear on the ballot in up to 194 local elections in 1994–95.

The unofficial list of jurisdictions in which petitions to place term limits on the ballot are possible, appears at the front of this book. Please note the caveat on the second page. All citizens interested in petitions to establish local term limits should consult with local counsel to determine the precise requirements of state and local laws affecting such efforts.

Two kinds of efforts are being made by Term Limits Everywhere! One is the straightforward petitions to place the issue on the ballot. This is going on in about 127 local jurisdictions (see Table J in the Technical Appendix). TLE! is a clearinghouse. It neither runs nor finances these local efforts. It does encourage them, but all the funding and work is done by local activists for limits.

Of these local efforts, one of the most interesting to watch may be the election for term limits for local officials in Spokane,

Washington. This is the heart of Speaker Tom Foley's district. Despite his die–hard opposition to term limits for elected officials, he will probably keep a low profile in this election, while term limits cruise to a strong victory among "his" voters.

The second effort of TLE! is to encourage local officials on their own to vote for term limits and place them on their ballots to become binding, charter amendments. Lobbying efforts are under way for this purpose in 67 additional cities. Some of these will succeed. In many, however, local officials may resist the idea, and petition efforts to get limits on the 1995 ballots may take place in these jurisdictions also.

Some of the statewide term limits efforts have an impact on local elections. Some include provisions for limits on all elected officials within the state, including local officials. Where this has been done, the initiatives include an "opt–out" provision, allowing any local jurisdiction whose citizens consider term limits unnecessary for them, to vote them down by majority vote in a general election.

The purpose of the opt–out is to avoid imposing limits in small jurisdictions where the problem is not officials who stay too long, but instead is persuading people to undertake the often low-paid and difficult work of running local governments.

By contrast, most of the elections to establish term limits at the local level have taken place in large cities, where budgets are large, special interests are powerful, and incumbents stay on forever with the assistance of those special interests.

Seventeen states and the District of Columbia are represented on the Term Limits Everywhere! lists. Some states, as the list in front notes, provide absolutely no opportunity for petitions to put term limits on the ballot — none statewide, and none in any local jurisdictions. Several more provide only severely limited opportunities for such citizen initiatives.

The states where the most number of such elections are likely are New York and New Hampshire. In New York, 32 jurisdictions are involved, including Albany, Buffalo, Ithaca, Poughkeepsie, Schenectady, Westchester County and Yonkers. Half of these are petitioning jurisdictions, half are lobbying jurisdictions (for now).

In New Hampshire, 21 jurisdictions are involved, but all are lobbying efforts. So, most of these will probably require later petitions and won't make the ballot until 1995.

Selected larger jurisdictions include Green Bay, Madison and Milwaukee in Wisconsin, Seattle and Spokane in Washington, Knoxville, Knox County and Nashville in Tennessee, Cleveland and Columbus in Ohio, Minneapolis and St. Paul in Minnesota (though the state's attorney general has cropped up with a hostile opinion letter on limits), Baltimore and Baltimore County in Maryland, Kansas City and Topeka in Kansas, Clearwater and Ft. Lauderdale in Florida, Burbank and Sacramento in California, and Washington, D.C.

The comparisons of term limits at the state and local levels with projections of how they would apply in Congress show that the effects of limits are not identical across the board. To the contrary, the need for limits and the effects of them are much stronger in large district elections than in small ones. The need for and the effects of limits are also stronger in governments with large budgets, that is in states, and in cities with budgets larger than some states.

> ***The Newspaper Rule***
>
> If you're thinking of running for Congress, rise early and read the newspaper. If you don't find the incumbent's name in the obituaries, the court docket page, or the front page for a juicy scandal, forget it and go back to bed.

In large–sized, large–budgeted jurisdictions, the same equation operates as in elections for Congress. Well–organized special interests count on incumbents to get what they want. Incumbents count on special interests to provide the campaign money so they can get reelected. The money and the media time it buys create a self–fulfilling prophecy — incumbents get reelected. And the beat goes on.

There is one indirect effect from term limits established at the local and state levels, on the eventual establishment of limits for Congress. In Illinois, for instance, the state constitution permits an initiative to create limits for the state legislature but doesn't permit an initiative for limits on Congress. (This assumes that the recent trial court decision taking away the opportunity of the people of Illinois to vote on this issue will be reversed in the Illinois Supreme Court.)

Once Illinois limits the terms of its state legislators, they will, in turn, have practical incentives to limit the terms of the state's congressional delegation. The same logic applies wherever local or state limits are created by law, instead of initiative.

Pending the final decision on the test case in the US Supreme Court, congressional limits can be established by law passed by state legislatures rather than by initiative. The only state that has acted so far is Utah, which passed a statute putting 12–year limits on state and federal officials. This was a defensive move by that legislature to defuse the term limits effort there. It failed; real term limits on local, state and federal officials will be on the Utah ballot, come November. The citizens of Utah do not want fig–leaf term limits.

Three other states which do not have citizen initiative provisions came close to enacting term limits by statute in 1993. In New Hampshire, New Jersey and Texas, one house of the legislature voted for genuine term limits as part of the election laws, but the other house killed the measure in two of them.

In New Hampshire, the house passed limits handily, the senate by a one–vote margin attached killer amendments. Limits died in the house on a procedural vote. If the Senate President Ralph Hough is defeated in the September primary by Representative Thomas Houlahan, as now seems likely, term limits will pass promptly in New Hampshire.

In New Jersey, limits also passed handily in the house. The Senate President Donald deFrancesco promised a floor vote which seemed likely to succeed. But, the Senate President reneged on his promise over a dispute concerning an Armenian holiday, and the measure died with the close of the session. Because of legislative membership changes, prospects for term limits in New Jersey are now cloudy.

In Texas, the House State Affairs Committee released multiple term limits bills to the floor. A majority of all members then voted in favor of one bill or another, but not a majority for any one bill. This outcome was probably deliberate.

Utah put a provision in its law which other states have copied. It provided that its law would not go into effect until at least 24 other states had acted on federal term limits. This provision offers no problem to limits and is welcomed by term limit supporters. After the Mississippi vote in 1995, all 23 states capable of establishing limits by initiative will have acted. Only two more states will be needed to cover half of the Senate by definition and half of the House depending on whether the two more states have 31 or more congressmen between them.

If, as expected, the voters of Illinois place limits on the tenure of their state legislators, those legislators will have an incentive to pass a law placing limits on the state's senators and representatives.

The first incentive is simple logic. New state legislators elected under term limits will believe in term limits, because they cannot be anything other than citizen legislators — coming to Springfield to serve for a few years and then move on. Those legislators will also have a personal stake in limits for Congress.

All state senators and most state representatives dream in their heart of hearts of becoming some day a member of the House of Representatives. Being limited themselves in Illinois and in other states, they cannot wait for the ideal opportunity to seek promotion — when the incumbent in their district dies, gets convicted or gets caught in a particularly noteworthy scandal.

The chances for state legislators to earn promotion to Congress are obviously far better in a term–limited Congress than at present. The people want congressional limits because they are good for the nation. State legislators want congressional limits because they are good for their career opportunities. And there is no greater engine for civic change than when the public interest is identical to the self–interests of the legislators.

The same equation plays out between local and state elected officials. Local officials often dream of becoming state legislators. If the local officials are term–limited, they will be looking for opportunities to advance. If the state legislators are limited, more opportunities for promotion will be available.

The last connection between term limit efforts at the local, state and federal levels is in the minds of the voters. The more chances that voters have to consider and vote on term limits at the local and state levels, the more they will work for and support limits at the federal level.

7

"Loss of Clout?" *or* "Restoring Citizen Control?"

Term Limit Debate by Supporters and Opponents

The public debate on term limits has been going on nationally since 1990. Four years are a short time for most major issues to mature, but limits have grown to national stature more quickly than most others. The debate is usually framed by opponents as a potential "loss of experience and clout." By supporters it is described as "restoring citizen control."

Much of the debate is fact–free. The participants state their personal views as if they were graven in stone. Opponents like Speaker Foley, being long–time successful members of Congress, expect deference from the citizenry. They believe they are right because they have been surrounded so long by people who say they are right.

> ***The Press Release Proof***
>
> Any politician who has reached the point of believing his own press releases is too out of touch to be trusted with power.

Many of the logical claims and counterclaims are covered at the end of this chapter in the Questions and Answer section. Beyond logic is the invective that term limits bring out. Their greatest opponent at the state level is probably Willie Brown, Speaker of the California Assembly. He called them the "worse move ever taken" by state voters. He also called Los Angeles County Supervisor Pete Schabarum, who led the effort for limits, "one of the most evil people to walk the face of the earth," as quoted in the Sacramento *Daily Recorder* in August, 1993.

Congressman Al Swift of Washington, a long–time colleague of Speaker Foley, appeared on "Capitol Newsbeat" from D.C. in a debate with Ed Crane of CATO Institute on November 2, 1991. About term limits, Congressman Swift said, people are "so frustrated that they will voluntarily give up their rights. There is a parallel here with Nazi Germany...."

Term limits have also generated an unusually strong opposition from political scientists, who are using invective as a substitute for investigation. Nelson Polsby called limits "constitutional mischief." Ross K. Baker called them, "quack therapy for democracy." Thomas Cronin described them as "an illusory quick fix for a symptom rather than a cure."

An article by Mark Petracca, cited in the Bibliography, suggests this hostility among political scientists is due to two factors — they tend to be liberals, and view limits as a conservative end–run. They tend to be comfortable working with the system as is. Net result, they are hostile to limits as a potentially upsetting influence on politics as now known and practiced.

Most of the opponents of term limits center their arguments on the untested assumption that the new breed of congressmen under limits will be lesser people with lesser legislative skills, than the veterans forced out by limits. The boldest, most colorful, but utterly untested such statement is from Norman Ornstein: "Only bums will run, only bums will rule." Yet there is one factual way to examine the nature of Congress if term limits applied. It is to take actual votes in Congress, and determine what changes would occur in those votes if the only members present and able to vote on them were those who would not be term–limited.

What If Congress was Term–Limited?
Effects on Four Actual Votes

Assume that term limits in the most common form, three terms for House and two for Senate, were in full effect as of 1992. A total of 53 senators and 233 representatives would therefore have been excluded. There is no magic to this; anyone, including a credentialed political scientist, can look at a calendar and verify this fact.

The first result is that in proportion to their members in the House and Senate, more Republicans than Democrats would be excluded by term limits. The second result is that the entire leadership of both the House and the Senate in both political parties would be forcibly retired. But whether that would mean worse government, or better, requires further exploration.

What would a term–limited Congress do in behalf of the public, with specific, major issues? There is an easy way to test the answer. Use actual votes to "replace" present members of both houses who would be excluded by limits, with new members to maintain the existing proportions of Republicans and Democrats in both houses. (Of course, there is no guarantee that party members would be replaced, one for one. But this allows a fair comparison between what actually happened and what in theory would happen.)

Next, give the replacement members the same voting habits as the remaining, nonlimited members of their own party in their own house. In other words, if 40 percent of the short–term House Democrats voted for a tax cut, and 100 new Democrats are added, then 40 of them would vote for the tax cut.

This process was applied to four critical votes in the first year of the Clinton administration. They were the $16 billion stimulus package, the president's budget, NAFTA and the Penny–Kasich $97 billion spending reduction plan.

In the House dominated by long–term representatives, the joint positions of Speaker Foley and President Clinton prevailed in all four of these votes. The smallest of these in economic impact was the $16 billion stimulus plan in the Clinton administration's first year. It passed the House, but was defeated by a filibuster in the Senate (failure to obtain 40 votes to close debate).

The stimulus plan would have passed in a term-limited House also. But the three other major administration issues would all have gone the other way, with major consequences for the American taxpayers and workers. Here are the particulars:

The president's budget passed the House by 218–216, a margin of only one vote, since in Congress a tie is a loss. It then went on to pass the Senate, 51–50, with Vice President Gore casting the tie–breaking vote.

Among representatives serving less than six years, however, the vote on the budget was a 94–108 *loss.* If the House had been term–limited, the president's budget would have suffered a resounding, 203–231 loss.

The Penny–Kasich spending reduction plan was a bipartisan effort to cut $97 billion from the budget, months after the president's budget had passed. It was developed by Tim Penny (D, Minn., 1st) and John Kasich (R, Ohio, 12th), and followed up on the promise of both President Clinton and Speaker Foley that an opportunity to make additional cuts would be forthcoming. However, when Penny–Kasich was proposed, both the administration and Speaker Foley adamantly opposed it. It lost in the House, 216–219. There was no Senate vote on the proposal.

The change, if the House had been term–limited, is dramatic. It would have voted for Penny–Kasich, 246–188. The principal difference between short–term House members and long–term ones is this — short–termers prefer to cut the deficit by cutting spending. Long–termers prefer to cut the deficit by raising taxes, as in the president's budget. In this choice the short–termers accurately reflect the current views of the American people. The long–termers represent the views the people had two decades ago, which makes sense when one notes that the average House leader was elected 25 years ago.

Tim Penny is also known for the fact that he has announced his retirement. He is relatively young, well respected, and probably would have been easily reelected. But, after six terms, he chose to leave, and commented, "Too many people come to Washington and stay too long."

The third major vote that would have changed is NAFTA (the North American Free Trade Agreement). After a bitter, national fight which split the House Democratic leadership leaving only Speaker Foley backing the president's position, the House voted for NAFTA, 234–200. Had the House been term–limited, the vote would have been 220–214, apparently still a victory for the president's position.

But, the short–term Democrats were the strongest group against NAFTA. They voted 90–168 against it. And, with term limits, Speaker Foley would have been gone. The short–term Democrats would have picked a different Speaker, logically one who shared their nearly 2–1 opposition to NAFTA, someone with views like Democratic Majority Whip David Bonior (D, Mich., 10th) who led the fight against NAFTA.

Any Speaker of the House who lacks the capacity to swing more than six votes his or her way on a blood–and–guts issue like NAFTA, lacks the political skills to become Speaker in the first place. So NAFTA would have lost in a term–limited House.

Although some commentators charge that term–limits are a plot to replace Democrats with Republicans, in these three critical votes for the Clinton administration, the difference in Republican votes had nothing to do with the difference in the results. It is true, as a study by the National Taxpayers Union demonstrates, that all members of Congress tend to become more free–spending the longer they stay in Washington. This happens to both Democrats and Republicans, though the margin between the two parties remains as both sides move up the tax–and–spend scale.

In a term–limited House, the Republican side would generate a few more votes against high spending and large government than at present. But the shifts on the Republican side are minor and in none of these votes would have changed the outcome.

In each instance, the margin of defeat for a Democratic administration would have been on the Democratic side of the aisle. The "old" Democrats heavily favor higher taxes and larger government as a solution to all problems. This includes President Clinton, who has re–earned his spurs as an "old" Democrat, now that he is safely ensconced in the White House.

"New" Democrats, like the American people themselves, have long since abandoned this view of the proper function of the federal government. That is the critical reason why a term–limited Congress would better reflect the will of the people than does the present Congress. In short, if the "old" Democrats were "rotated out of office" as described in Chapter 5, the public policies in the United States would be radically different, and much more in line with current opinion of the people.

Much the same results occurred in California after the 1992 elections for its legislature. After term limits survived their last legal challenge, one–quarter of all its 40 senators and 80 assemblymen, resigned to take various full–time jobs elsewhere, many as lobbyists in Sacramento. Not only could almost all of them have won — in fact, three of them did win and then resigned. One stayed long enough to vote Willie Brown in as Speaker again, and resigned the next day. (See, *The California Legislature,* page 79.)

The new breed of legislators in California turned out to be "new" Democrats, not replacement Republicans. The factual experience in California suggests the same result as the theoretical analysis of four US House votes, above. Instead of substituting incompetent amateurs for seasoned veterans and impeding the business of government, the opposite happened. Government functions better when the "experience" of elected representatives is not confined to perpetual reelection and perpetual inability to solve the problems of the day.

This leads to the common issues raised and charges made about term limits. There are many myths and few facts in the public debate now under way on the subject. The following Question and Answer section deals with most of these.

In public and academic debates, in conversations and on talk radio shows, the same questions and comments tend to come up from both supporters and opponents of term limits. These are in this format for the benefit of readers who expect to participate in debates on the merits of term limits on talk shows, to write Op–Ed articles or letters to the editor, and so forth.

Questions and Answers on Term Limits

Q: Don't term limits automatically mean a loss of experience in Congress (or in any other legislative body)?

A: The experience with governors and with recent California legislative elections shows that people elected under term limits have long work experience — but in the private sector or other governments, rather than in the same office for decades.

Q: Regardless of length of experience, don't limits mean a loss of clout for states whose members of Congress have seniority?

A: If only one state limited its members of Congress, this would be true. However, after the election of 1994, almost 50 percent of both the House and the Senate will be limited. Together with members who believe in limits even if their states have not yet acted, a majority of both houses should support limits. At this point, the seniority system will be abolished, and length of service as a source of clout for any district will end.

Q: Aren't term limits undemocratic, because they prevent voters from voting for whom they choose?

A: If congressional elections were open and competitive, this would be true. But they aren't, and haven't been for more than 60 years. The reelection rate of incumbent House members this time will match again its all–time high of 98 percent in 1988. There is no real competition now.

This charge made by opponents of term limits is a cry to lock the barn door after the horse is stolen. And the hypocrisy is that the thieves who stole democracy from the people — the long–term incumbents — are the very ones pushing this argument.

Besides, there is nothing "undemocratic" about the people deciding by an average margin of 67 percent in favor, that they need and want term limits to reestablish competition in elections for Congress (or for any other offices).

Q: Don't the people have a right to elect anyone they want to public office, even someone who has served in that office many terms before?

A: Of course they do, if that was what was going on. Given the advantages of incumbency and self–established perks of Congress, there is no choice whatsoever. The people are going to get the incumbent again until he/she is dead, disabled, or imprisoned. That is called a Hobson's Choice — take what you are offered or get nothing at all.

Besides, under many of the term limit proposals, an incumbent who is barred now can come back in two years (House) or six years (Senate) and run again. That sort of political hopscotch has happened only in two sets of governor's races (Alabama and Ohio) in 50 years.

How rare this is, demonstrates the false premise. Incumbents don't survive by choice, just by compulsion.

Q: People like Speaker of the House Tom Foley say we "already have term limits," because the people can "vote me out every two years if they wish." Isn't this true?

A: This wheezy chestnut is another wrinkle on the last two questions. Speaker Foley and all the other long–term incumbents work long and hard (and their staffs do also) to make certain they face no serious opposition for reelection. Their goal is to scare off significant opposing candidates by gathering unmatchable war chests from special interests, up to a year before the election.

Residents of Speaker Foley's Spokane, Washington, district have as much chance of defeating him in any election as a farm boy just off the turnip truck has of beating a card shark in Las Vegas. This is a false argument. Speaker Foley, more than anyone else in Washington, DC, knows it is false, works to make it false, and counts on it being false.

Q: If members are term–limited, but their staffs are not limited, doesn't that mean more of government will be in the hands of nonelected people?

A: The average congressman has a staff of about 35 people. Anyone who cannot control and direct a staff of that size has no business being elected to help run a government with over three million employees.

Every member of a congressional staff serves at the pleasure of the member and can be dismissed at any time for any reason, including mere political disagreement. A member who cannot control the actions of others under those circumstances is a pathetic excuse for a manager.

Q: Even if the congressman can control his own staff, what about the bureaucrats? They were there before he got there and will be there when he's gone.

A: The "iron triangle" is the relationship between bureaucrats, special interests, and the committees that allegedly oversee their area of interest. At present, this incestuous relationship governs much of what Congress does. That situation will be better once congressmen are elected who have neither the time nor the tolerance for business as usual.

Also, Congress authorizes, defines the job, and pays the salary for every single bureaucrat employed by the federal government. If Congress cannot control the bureaucrats, it means Congress cannot control its own laws.

Q: Won't term limits discourage the best leaders from running for high public office?

A: To the contrary, the present seniority system causes people to wait 25 years for a chance to run a committee (like Sam Gibbons of Florida, who held his hat in his hand for 25 years before taking over for Dan Rostenkowski). In the real world, the kind of people who *ought* to run for Congress are not the type to wait a quarter of a century before getting a responsible position.

Q: Doesn't it take many years to gain the knowledge to guide the destinies of a "corporation" as large as the federal government, and aren't the members of Congress essentially the "board of directors" of the world's most complex "corporation?"

A: Leaders of Congress sometimes say that many years are needed for precisely this reason. Yet, the CEOs (Chief Executive Officers) of the Fortune 500, the nation's largest businesses, employ more people and handle more funds than do the 535 members of Congress. Average tenure of the CEOs of large corporations is 9.1 years, compared to

24.0 years for the leaders of Congress, and 12.4 for all congressmen. Obviously, it doesn't take that many years, or the congressmen are very slow learners.

Q: *What will happen to women and minorities if term limits are established? Won't they lose their hard–fought gains in representation in the last few decades?*

A: Absolutely not. The experience with the California legislative elections in 1992 showed a one–third gain in women in the assembly and senate, and gains for racial minorities. Term limits will not totally eradicate the elderly, white male dominance of American politics, but it will make a dent in that partial monopoly.

Q: *If members are limited to only two or three terms, doesn't that mean they'll be more likely to sell out to the special interests, including those that offer them jobs after service in Congress?*

A: The present situation is that members have already sold out to the special interests in order to keep their present jobs forever. Limits will put in office people who are less beholden to the special interests, ones who know that Congress will not be their entire lives, ones who know there was life before Congress and will be life afterward. Such congressmen will be less likely to sell out to the special interests.

Q: *Rather than take the risks of term limits, isn't public funding the way to solve the incumbency advantage?*

A: Public funding — even if voters approved of it, which they very much do not — won't solve the problem. Incumbents have an advantage of 5 to 15 percent of the votes before the polls open. If challengers somehow had equal money, they would still lose in droves because of the incumbency advantage.

Q: Wouldn't we lose the advantage of the services of great and able legislators by limiting the terms to two or three?

A: People of exceptional ability rise to the top in any competitive environment. The reverse could just as well be true; senators or representatives who might have been more honest or able presidents than Nixon or Carter, for instance, never ran for president and stayed buried in the House or Senate to take advantage of their hard– and long–earned seniority.

Term limits would encourage people of ability to seek promotion, as in the military where the process is "up or out." The military is one of the best examples in all of American society where the most able people rise to the top, without regard to race, sex, or national origin.

Q: Once Congress is term–limited, won't that shift power from the legislative branch to the president?

A: The present congressmen, especially the leaders, are more concerned with hanging onto their positions of power and the perks that go with it, than they are in getting the substantive business of the nation accomplished. Power has already shifted from Congress to the president. It will shift back when a new breed of congressmen arrives, ones who are pragmatic and who know they have only six years to do the jobs for which they were elected.

The Constitution gives Congress ample power, since it controls the purse strings and writes all the laws under which the executive branch employees are hired and fired. A do–nothing Congress wastes this power. A go–get–'em Congress will use this power wisely, as the people want.

Also, keep in mind that presidents are already term–limited. There is no reason why a term–limited Congress would not operate on an even basis with such presidents.

Q: Aren't long–termers so secure in their positions that special interests can no longer "purchase" their loyalty? Wouldn't short–termers be more vulnerable to the special interests?

A: Special interests currently "purchase" congressmen not only through those who receive their donations, but through those who don't. Special interests (PACs) give about 10 times as much to incumbents as to challengers. If elections were more competitive — which is the principal advantage of term limits — special interests would have to give to challengers as well, since they might wind up winning. And when special interests are compelled by their own selfish concerns to donate to both candidates, they wind up owning neither of them.

Q: Wouldn't a law requiring federally regulated TV stations to give free time to all candidates for Congress go a long way toward solving the problem, without term limits?

A: Perhaps it would, but there is one big impediment, the First Amendment. Under freedom of the press no law can tell any newspaper what to print or not to print. If push comes to shove, the broadcast media will win on that point, or they will win on the point of taking property without just compensation, since selling time on the air is the only property that any broadcaster possesses.

Whether or not this might work is irrelevant. As long as we have the First Amendment, it is impossible.

Q: Even if term limits that require an incumbent to sit out a term might be effective and constitutional, how can a lifetime ban be constitutional?

A: Whatever the Constitution says in its text by definition is constitutional. For instance, having two senators each for Wyoming and California clearly violates the principle of "one man, one vote." However, that provision is in the Constitution, so it is constitutional. The 22nd Amendment is a lifetime ban against anyone serving as president more than two terms. It is constitutional. So will be a similar amendment concerning members of Congress.

Q: If seniority is ended as a method of selecting leaders in Congress, won't that produce a greedy free–for–all among all members to seek the leadership positions in each new Congress?

A: Henry Clay was elected Speaker of the House on the same day he was sworn in as a member. Intelligent men and women have ways of figuring out in small groups who their best people might be — those with leadership potential. Just like a jury in which every member has the theoretical right to be named as foreman, Congress will also be able to find its own leaders — and they will be chosen for merit, not just for years of survival.

Q: Won't term limits make congressmen the slaves of their constituents, forced by changing tides of public opinion to do whatever constituents currently demand, instead of exercising mature judgment as present members do?

A: The question assumes that present congressmen have the time and space to exercise their "judgment" as Edmund Burke said they should. They do not; they are slaves to the special interests who hold their purse strings. Term–limited members will discover, like legislators from time immemorial, there are only a few issues about which the public cares passionately. Most issues are of less interest to the public; on those, members can exercise their judgment. The vote for the War in the Gulf showed that voters will respect their representatives for whatever judgment they exercise, when the chips are down and reason can lead to either conclusion.

Q: Aren't term limits just a disguised effort by conservatives and Republicans to knock out of office liberal Democrats who keep winning reelection?

A: In California legislative elections in 1992, term limits caused one–quarter of the legislature to resign for other jobs. Most who left were Democrats. Republicans did not gain members in that legislature; they lost one (essentially a tie). The present Congress shows a similar pattern. If two–term and three–term limits were applied to the present Congress, a greater proportion of the Republicans than the Democrats would be forced out of office.

The people who really fear term limits are the long–term officeholders. Republican leaders in Congress have cooperated with Democrats in keeping term limits from serious consideration, because *all* the Republican and Democratic leaders would be equally forced out by limits.

There is currently no difference between Republican and Democratic leaders of Congress on the subject of term limits. Both sets of leaders oppose them, though the Republicans are quiet in their opposition. All the leaders are out of touch with their constituents, since polls demonstrate that rank and file Republicans and Democrats strongly support term limits.

8

An Idea Whose Time Has Come?

Progress of Term Limits to Date

The term limits effort is fueled by the chronic inability of Congress to come to grips with critical questions of its own behavior and, as a result, by the growing public support for term limits and for the specific "3 and 2 Plan" (three terms in the House, two in the Senate), as described in Chapter 4. Both trends apply also to those state legislatures with a long history of entrenched incumbents, and also to those city and county governments with the same perceived problem.

What will be the combined effect of these related trends in the election of 1994?

Because petition drives are still under way as this is written, the precise number of jurisdictions where the people will vote on term limits cannot be known. It is known from experience that supporters of limits usually are able to gather 35 percent more signatures than the number required, which is enough to deal with the "shrinkage," the loss of signatures for various reasons as election officials verify the petitions.

Also, it is not uncommon for term limits opponents to file suit to knock such issues off the ballot on various grounds. Experience shows that courts will seldom knock out petitions before an election, but will reserve judgment and may knock them out after they have been approved by the voters. Exactly that occurred in Arkansas and Nebraska this year.

The Arkansas Supreme Court case, discussed elsewhere, upheld limits on all state officials but struck them down as applied to members of Congress. That is the test case, now in the US Supreme Court.

An even greater challenge faced petitioners for limits in the District of Columbia. Due to the vagaries of DC election laws, petitioners had only five days to gather 16,000 signatures to make the November 1994 ballot in DC. Petitioning in DC is harder than any other jurisdiction because so many of the people found in public places are not residents, and because the registration level of those who are residents is relatively low.

For those reasons, the target in DC was set at 32,000 signatures to make sure enough valid ones would remain after the checking process of names and current addresses. The formal announcement came in August; term limits for District officials will be on the November ballot. No other issue or candidate has ever gathered so many signatures in DC in such a short period of time. The success of many other petition drives can be classified as major achievements, but the result in DC was a political miracle, never matched in any other jurisdiction for any purpose.

Limits are also likely to become an issue in the District election in November, since incumbent Mayor Sharon Pratt Kelly supports them, but one of her opponents, former Mayor (and former inmate) Marion Barry, opposes them.

In Mississippi, the petitions being gathered now cannot put the issue on the 1994 ballot due to that state's two–stage requirement. Initiatives there must go to the legislature first for consideration, before they go on the ballot. There is no question, however, that limits either will be passed by the Mississippi legislature, or will go on the 1995 ballot.

Therefore, this is the status of statewide initiative efforts, including those which are under way now but may not make the ballot until 1995: 11 statewide (including DC as a state for these purposes) are currently under way and should succeed. That will exhaust the list of states with the power of initiative. DC and Illinois are acting only on limits for local officials. Illinois law does not permit an initiative for federal officials, so only nine states are acting on congressional terms.

These nine states will be added to the 15 states that have already acted in 1990 and 1992, though the 15 prior states were temporarily reduced to 14 through the unfortunate but temporary setback from the Nebraska Supreme Court.

Although the people of Illinois cannot vote directly on limits for Congress, a term–limited Illinois legislature will have strong incentives, both public and personal, to pass statutes that limit its congressional delegation. Either of two political incentives can produce this result. One is, "I'll do unto you as they did unto me." The other is that as soon as a citizen becomes a freshman representative from Elephant Breath, Illinois, in his heart of hearts he is dreaming of becoming a congressman. Both incentives lead to the same conclusion, congressional term limits by law in Illinois.

Also of those 23 jurisdictions, 21 have already established, or will establish in the elections coming up, limits on their own legislatures. Limits on terms of governors are the most common, with 41 states now having or about to have, limits in place for that office. This counts the mayor of DC as a governor, being the chief executive officer of a jurisdiction as large and at least as complex as many states.

It is harder to assess the general pattern of local initiatives for several reasons. The first is the patchwork quilt of positions being taken by the city or county attorneys who usually review all initiatives and advise the counsels on their legal definitions and adequacy. In Wisconsin, for instance, a total of 16 different local petitions are under way in various stages. Even though the initiative law is statewide, and should apply the same way in all jurisdictions, in some cities the city attorneys have ruled the initiative suitable for the ballot. In others, they have dug in their heels, have ruled the initiatives improper and are resisting them, presumably at the behest of long-time councilmen who would prefer that the people not vote on this issue.

The second difficulty in assessing the general pattern of local initiatives is date of relevant elections. Local elections frequently are not on the same schedule as state elections, or national ones, or both. In addition, local laws sometimes provide for special elections to vote on initiatives, depending on the time until the next general election, when the signatures are filed.

So, it is impossible to say whether many of the local initiatives will be voted on in 1994 or 1995, much less whether they will coincide with the federal election in November 1994. However, the gathering of signatures to place limits on local ballots is meeting with the same level of public acceptance and willingness to sign as the statewide petitions have experienced generally in the past.

In summary, efforts already under way will place limits for state or federal office or both on 11 state ballots and in DC in 1994–95. Limits should pass in every such jurisdiction, with the closest vote anticipated in DC. Since the New York City initiative in 1993 showed that both Democrats and black voters favored term limits, the expected outcome in DC should approach the 60 percent to 40 percent victory in New York City.

And efforts already under way will place limits on local ballots, both limiting terms of local officials and putting local voters on record as demanding state and federal limits in a total of 23 states, and about 190 local jurisdictions.

A list of best information on state and local term limit initiatives appears in the Technical Appendix as Table J.

As of 1995, all that can be accomplished through statewide initiatives will have been completed. Local initiatives on limits will continue, as court challenges are successful, and as the word spreads to more people in more places that such is even possible. The success rate in local initiatives is not expected to be 100 percent as it is in statewide campaigns. In the smaller towns, the problem is less often elected officials serving forever, than getting people to agree to serve.

Also, the disconnection between voters and elected officials tends to increase in proportion to increasing size of the jurisdiction. For both reasons, there will be a significant minority of local elections where voters decide that term limits might be useful at the state and federal levels, but aren't necessary in South Succotash.

All the successes in statewide and local campaigns will not put congressional term limits over the top, by themselves. The statewide elections will mean that 46 senators, therefore 46 percent of the Senate, will be subject to limits when these elections are completed. It will also mean, given the number of representatives of the states involved, that 183 members of the House, or 42.8 percent. will also be limited.

These numbers will bring the national effort close to success but not over the top. The next steps, which will ensure universal success, are described in Chapter 11.

9

War in the Trenches — Strategy and Tactics of Supporters *and* Opponents of Term Limits

Although the drive for term limits is quite short compared to all other efforts to obtain major constitutional change, common characteristics have appeared in campaigns to date. Certain organizations have cropped up repeatedly as participants on one side or the other.

Likewise, the grand strategy and specific tactics used by both supporters and opponents have demonstrated common characteristics. All these common qualities in prior campaigns are likely in future term limit campaigns.

The organization most involved in term limit campaigns is US Term Limits. Other organizations that specialize in limits include Americans Back in Charge, Term Limits Legal Institute, and Americans to Limit Congressional Terms. National organizations that include limits on their agenda and work for them, include Citizens Against Government Waste, National Taxpayers Union, and United We Stand America. Also, every active state has a local organization like ACTIV in California, and "Eight is Enough" in Florida.

There is no single major organization opposing term limits. But, opposing organizations more than make up in numbers and in dollars committed and spent, for their lack of a dominant single one. Among the consistent opponents of term limits are local, state and federal employee unions, the tobacco industry, major public utilities, and lawyers, especially trial lawyers and lobbyists.

Not all jurisdictions require that campaign contributions for or against initiative campaigns be publicly declared, nor are reporting requirements as rigorously enforced as they are through the Federal Election Commission for contributions to campaigns of federal officials. Therefore, accurate national summaries of total financial participation of supporters and opponents cannot be made. *Partial* information involving contributions of $5,000 and up in such campaigns in prior years by opponents is reported in Table A in the Technical Appendix.

The strategy of term limit supporters is easily stated, get the issue on the ballot and count on the people to vote in favor once given the opportunity. As a result of the well–funded media campaigns conducted against term limits in California, Michigan and Washington State, a second strategy was also developed. Be prepared with money and professional assistance to counterattack when the opponents attack on television.

The strategy of term limit opponents is equally well stated. Do and say nothing while the petition campaign is under way, in hopes it will not raise the required number of signatures. Once term limits have the signatures, organize quickly and raise funds quickly. Use the most powerful incumbent spokesmen within the state to try to sell the idea of "loss of clout," and loss of "experience" and "institutional memory."

At the same time, attack in court both before the election in an effort to prevent the vote, and afterward to have the results thrown out.

The most interesting overall point is that *both* supporters and opponents operate on the same central assumption — if the people get to make the decision on term limits they will support them. The only exception to that rule is the first vote in Washington State for reasons described in Chapter 1. Since that problem was corrected in the second vote there a year later and will not be repeated, the strategy of both sides will continue to assume the voters will approve limits.

In a few short years but many major elections, the tactics of both sides have changed somewhat as they adapt to experiences. Supporters of limits have changed more. Opponents of limits have stuck mainly with the tactics they first used in Washington State in 1991, even though those tactics succeeded once, but since have led to an unbroken series of losses.

In Washington State in 1991, opponents mounted a last–minute, expensive and high–profile TV ad campaign. It presented one major theme, that the people of the state would lose influence in Washington. The voice–over announcer said, "we'll shoot ourselves in the foot" if we approve term limits.

It offered two major examples of the results of this, that the people would lose their Social Security and that the water of the Columbia River would be diverted to California. It also presented the subplot that term limits are driven by sinister "Eastern" interests, apparently seeking to take over Washington State.

The loss of Social Security theme disappeared from later campaigns in Washington and elsewhere. However, the loss of water theme continues. In Michigan, the ads said that water would be siphoned from the Great Lakes to be sent elsewhere, without saying where. In Arkansas, the ads said that state water would be piped into Texas. (Apparently there's no love lost between Arkansans and Texans.)

It is unclear to supporters of term limits why their opponents think they are fronting for a shadowy gang of "Hungarian water jugglers," to quote "The Muppet Show." However, the claim is so patently absurd that supporters replied with a TV ad in Arkansas that repeated the charge, showed a mournful basset hound, and used the voice–over, "That dog won't hunt."

Michigan also introduced another theme, ominous music over a picture of workers in radiation suits, and the claim that if term limits passed, the state would become a dumping ground for waste from all other states. Based on the decision of the voters in all these jurisdictions, none of those dogs would hunt.

The opponents' Nebraska ad had a new wrinkle. It showed a burning American flag with a voice–over about "losing our right to vote." Apparently the creators of the ad, who didn't come from Nebraska, did not understand that Nebraskans don't take kindly to the picture of a US flag being burned.

The last tactic of the opponents is to ignore the issue of term limits itself, and attack instead the people who give money to the issue. They are attacked as outsiders and as "Libertarians." The goal is to get the press to focus on these outsiders, and pay less attention to the fact that hundreds of thousands of state residents, millions in large states like California and Florida, want term limits and are willing to vote for, work for, or even donate money to the effort to get them.

At the same time, the opponents finance their campaigns with big–ticket contributions from corporations or organizations that have little or no direct connection to that state or that issue in that state. The only connection is that the person asking for the contribution is a powerful incumbent with the capacity to hurt that corporation real bad or help it real good. Sometimes the request for a check comes from the politically active and visible wife of such an incumbent, as with Speaker Foley and with Congressman John Dingell (D, Mich., 16th), who is Chairman of the Energy and Commerce Committee.

In the past, supporters have not got the press to focus on both the tactics used to raise money for antilimits campaigns and the sources of that money. This will change in the campaigns of 1994. Supporters think that the public has a right to know what is happening, when they pop open a Miller Genuine Draft, fire up a Marlboro, dip an Oreo Cookie in milk, heat up a Kraft macaroni and cheese dinner, turn on their electric lights in Southern California, pay taxes to employ a bureaucrat or hire a teacher, or hire a trial lawyer, to name a few examples. When people do these things, they are sending part of their money to Michigan and other states to fight against term limits for Congress.

In the early campaigns, term limit supporters assumed, naively, that all they had to do was get the issue on the ballot and truth and justice would prevail from there. In more recent campaigns, they have learned as Paul Jacob, Executive Director of US Term Limits, said, to save some money and "be prepared to go toe to toe on TV with the opposition in the last 70 days of the campaign."

The kind of campaigns to expect and the financing behind them are illustrated by the vote–no effort against state legislative limits in California in 1990.

The *Los Angeles Times* reported on October 31, 1990, the specific industries and the favors they were seeking in Sacramento, who had donated to the vote "no" campaigns on Propositions 131 and 140, the two term–limits proposals that were on the ballot that year in California (see Table A in the Technical Appendix). Much of the grand total of $3.3 million went into television advertising.

The television ads claimed, among other points, that "special interest groups and developers will amass even more power" if the limits pass. The opposition campaign cited "lawyers, real estate interests, and members of professional associations" as examples of these special interests. The irony is that lawyers, real estate interests, and professionals donated the money to make these claims against the term limit propositions. Trial lawyers and doctors are shown by name in the high–dollar list in the Technical Appendix. But one has to know Southern California to identify the Irvine Co. as a major land developer seeking new gasoline taxes and toll roads to provide better access to its marketable land.

Said Jim Weaton, campaign director for Yes on 131, "Every unsavory special interest is lining up with [Speaker] Willie Brown... Everyone with a stake in keeping the rules the same in Sacramento is giving." The biggest single contributor was the California Teachers Association, the union representing 220,000 California Teachers. Their executive director, Ralph Flynn, commented, "The reality is the legislative process with all its infirmities is really the best thing we have going for us."

The second largest contributor was the horse racing industry that wanted expanded satellite wagering on closed circuit out–of–state races. The third biggest donor was the tobacco industry. They wanted to prevent cigarette taxes from being spent on anti–smoking TV ads, and for the state to preempt local government efforts to regulate smoking.

The fourth largest contributor, and the last one to give more than $100,000, was lawyers. They wanted to block no–fault auto insurance and to prevent erosion of the right to sue for damages generally. A representative of the California Trial Lawyers remarked, "Obviously, it's a great advantage to have someone who is a champion of your cause as Speaker of the Assembly." To this, term limit supporters say today, it's also quite handy to have a powerhouse like Speaker Foley, Chairman Dingell, or any other controlling figure in Washington, DC, pushing your special interest, whatever it is.

It takes resources and expertise to dig out and report such a story. Term limits supporters don't have the resources to do it. TV news reporters, local or national, apparently lack either the will or the resources to do the job. So it is left to the major print media to report such stories, or they go unreported altogether. What such coverage demonstrates when it happens, however, is the blinding hypocrisy of term limits opponents. This is no better demonstrated than by lawyers donating money for a campaign that bashes lawyers as special interests to be feared by the public.

The last lesson to learn from the kinds of interests that contributed money against limits in California in 1990, and are again contributing money against limits in campaigns in 1994 concerns left–handed money. Both corporations and unions are barred by federal law from contributing directly to the election campaigns of all federal officials (congressional and presidential). However, corporations and unions *can* contribute money to initiative campaigns.

Is there any doubt that powerful congressmen are just as grateful for contributions to save their collective necks against limits as they are for contributions to their personal campaigns? Especially when the congressmen or their wives personally solicit these large–ticket contributions, it is clear that this left–handed money is intended for the same purpose as right–handed (campaign) contributions, to curry the favor of the congressmen in question.

There are two reasons for this long discussion of a single state campaign conducted four years ago. The first is to thank the *Los Angeles Times* for its hard–slogging research that put this story together. The other is to suggest that the same types of groups with the same types of back–room interests in legislative results are coming out of the woodwork everywhere an expensive, antilimits campaign occurs.

Opponents in the 1994–95 campaigns are expected to mount advertising attacks on "loss of clout" one more time. Supporters will reply, again, that dog won't hunt, especially since limits are about to apply to a majority in both houses of Congress.

There is no such thing in a legislative body that acts by majority vote, of the majority losing its clout to the minority.

Opponents are expected to claim, once again, that term limits mean "loss of institutional memory." Supporters will reply again that there are books on past history in Washington, DC, Springfield, Illinois, and every other jurisdiction that will be voting. Presumably, most newly elected representatives at any level can read, and therefore will obtain whatever history about their late, unlamented predecessors that they need.

Opponents are expected to claim, again, that term limits already exist, because the voters are "free to vote the incumbents out, at the next election." With substantial dollars behind such a campaign, it can make some headway.

For example: in August 1990 the California Poll by the widely–respected Field Institute showed much stronger support for term limits than appeared in the final vote. As reported in the *San Francisco Examiner,* September 7, 1990, on Prop. 140 (limits on state legislators), 67 percent supported it, 20 percent opposed it, and 13 percent were undecided. Yet, the final vote was 52 percent to 48 percent.

Either all of the undecideds chose the no vote eventually (plus many of the yes votes). Or, the high–powered campaign against Prop, 140 moved a substantial portion of the population against it, though not enough to defeat it

The poll also suggested both the weakest and strongest arguments used by opponents. Only 31 percent of respondents agreed with Speaker Willie Brown's statement that limits would produce "inexperienced legislators" who were "more easily manipulated by special interests." Only 36 percent agreed with his statement that limits are bad because "politicians need one or two terms to learn the job."

The strongest argument against limits, the one which Speaker Foley is using as often as possible today against congressional limits, is "A limit on terms is not needed because if voters don't like elected officials they can always vote them out of office." Forty–three percent of respondents agreed, and 53 percent disagreed, still a minority, but a significant one.

That statement is factually false, as discussed in Chapter 2, and demonstrated in Table B and Table E in the Technical Appendix. But since it is the only one of the opponents' arguments that comes close to attracting majority support. it will probably be a mainstay of their campaigns in 1994 and 1995.

The most sinister tactic of term limit opponents is to place pressure on term limit activists by threatening their jobs. In a few cases, leaders of term limits efforts who work for large corporations doing business with state governments, have been approached by their superiors and advised to leave the issue alone. Presumably, the message has been passed along verbally from powerful politicians through the government affairs office of the corporation, to the employees' bosses. This author will not name the employees and employers because it is not the intention to get people fired for doing their civic duty as they see fit. But, this tactic has been used in the past and unfortunately may happen again.

Interestingly, much of the political muscle being put into opposition to term limits comes not from congressmen, who are most often the targets of initiatives, but from state legislators who may fear that they are next. The logic is simple — once the public gets a taste for the blood of overripe incumbents, it won't stop at Congress. They are probably right in that assumption, especially in the larger states.

The major tactic of opponents, however, is to use the courts either to prevent the people from ever voting on the issue, or to throw out the results of the public judgment. Few if any attempts to prevent a vote taking place will succeed, now that the US Supreme Court has taken a test case on the issue. The usual response of a lower court once the Supreme Court takes up an issue, is to hold its fire and wait to hear the results.

The Oklahoma Supreme Court did just that in July 1994, holding off a ruling on the merits of a challenge to term limits but refusing to grant an injunction sought by opponents to prevent the 1994 vote.

The decision, also in July, of a trial court in Illinois to enjoin a vote there on limits for state legislators, may be reversed by the Illinois Supreme Court for the same reason, even though the Illinois court offered reasons for its decision under Illinois law, not under the US Constitution.

The organizing, fundraising, advertising and media efforts of the opponents will fail in 1994 almost universally, as they have in past.

> ***Acting Congressional***
> Dress like a congressman. Sound like a congressman. Talk at length and in complete sentences. But, never reach any conclusion harmful to your reelection donors.

The personalities will be different in future election campaigns. But a change of personalities does not mean the campaigns will be radically different. In general, term limits will win by a walk–over unless one or more dominant political figures take the lead in fighting against limits.

There are few qualities in common between Speaker of the House Tom Foley and Speaker of the California Assembly Willie Brown except both are Democrats and both hold immense and unquestioned power within their legislative domains. However, their power caused a similar result.

Both were able to put the bite on major corporations and unions to contribute heavily to the no campaign. And, both were able to depress the actual vote in their states far below the level of support for term limits reported by reputable, independent polls prior to the elections.

So, the largest factor in term limit elections is probably the presence, or absence, of a major political figure in that jurisdiction who is (a) extremely powerful, (b) untouchable for reelection in his/her district, and (c) adept at gaining support from major donors and from subordinate politicians who have been in the same office for a long time.

Where such a figure exists, he/she will have incentives to oppose term limits, and because of the safety of his/her own position will probably lead the fight against limits. Such figures can depress the support for limits, but cannot defeat them provided that opponents recognize all strategies, counter all tactics, and effectively use their natural advantages among the public. Where there is no such opponent, term limits will probably succeed by a wide margin.

In either instance, the last tactic of the opponents will be to seek to take away in the courts the victory on limits that has been won from the voters. Court cases will usually be filed *before* the election, but usually will not be decided until after the election. It is critical to supporters to design their petitions based on prior experience in other jurisdictions, and prior court cases upholding various provisions, to give opponents the minimum opening to prevail in such court challenges.

Strong and safe opponents can take the lead visibly in suing to overturn term limit victories, as Speaker Foley did in Washington State, and as Speaker Brown did in California. They are willing, in effect, to sue their own voters, because they know they can safely get away with such a tactic. Where such opponents are not present, it is a simple matter to get individuals claiming to be acting for themselves, or fellow-traveler organizations like the League of Women Voters, to bring the cases as stalking horses for the real parties whose interests are at stake.

Because legal strategy and tactics are a special category, and will be foreclosed almost entirely by a favorable decision on a test case in the Supreme Court, they are discussed in the next chapter, "The Word from Olympus."

10

The Word from Olympus

What Will the Supreme Court Decide?

There have been about 10 term limit cases to date, most of them in lower courts. The one present Supreme Court case on the subject which has foreclosed many challenges to term limit initiatives is *Legislature v. Eu,* 816 P 2d 1309, (1991), *cert. denied,* 112 S Ct 1292 (1992).

Laymen reading the previous paragraph should not panic. It means the California legislature, compelled by Speaker Brown, officially sued March Fong Eu, Secretary of State of California. Speaker Brown wanted a declaration that term limits placed on the legislature by Proposition 140 which had just passed, were unconstitutional. The California Supreme Court ruled in 1991 that limits were legal. Speaker Brown then insisted the case be taken to the US Supreme Court in 1992. That Court denied *certiorari,* which means it refused to hear the case and left standing the decision of the California Supreme Court.

A principal function of the US Supreme Court is to make the final decisions on questions of US constitutional law. By definition, there should not be opposite decisions on a single point of constitutional law from different courts around the country. And the question of whether an initiative limiting the terms of elected *state or local* representatives violates the First Amendment political rights of either voters or candidates had been addressed by many lower courts, prior to the *Eu* decision.

When the Supreme Court refuses to hear a case, it does not speak as clearly as when it takes a case and issues its own opinion. Still, by refusing to review the California decision, the Court accepted for California, and will probably accept for any other jurisdiction, the idea that all state and local governments can limit the terms of their own officials as they see fit. It also accepted the idea that what legislatures can do, citizens can also do, by using the initiative process wherever that is available.

So, the bottom line from the *Eu* decision is to foreclose any more cases that claim term limits on their face are a violation of the political freedoms under the First Amendment. It is especially appropriate that the Court should rule this way, since the First Amendment says, in part, "Congress shall make no law... abridging... the right of the people... to petition the Government for a redress of grievances." Since the Bill of Rights was added to the Constitution, petitions by citizens have occupied a preferred position in American political theory.

The idea that state initiatives can limit terms of local or state officials does not answer the next question, whether they can also limit the terms of senators and representatives elected from that state. Three lower court decisions have approached this question, two said no but did so with different logic. One ducked the large question in favor of a smaller and easily solvable question.

On June 20, 1994, the US Supreme Court granted the petition for *certiorari* to the Supreme Court of Arkansas in *US Term Limits v. Thornton,* the first test case on limits to get that far. In plain English, this means the US Supreme Court has voluntarily agreed to hear argument whether the Arkansas court was right or wrong in ruling that an Arkansas initiative cannot limit the terms of members of Congress from that state.

The fact that the Arkansas case was taken does not mean that cases against term limits in federal court in Washington State and in the Supreme Court of Oklahoma, are being ignored. For instance, *Brown v. Board of Education,* 1954, the most important desegregation case, was not just one case, but a combination of four cases. It took its name from the first one on which the Supreme Court granted *certiorari.*

The Washington case, has been briefed and argued in the US Ninth Circuit Court of Appeals and is pending decision. The Oklahoma case has been decided only on the preliminary issue; the court refused to grant an injunction to prevent the initiative from appearing on the ballot. Either of those cases may be consolidated later with *Thornton,* the first one in the door.

It is a sad commentary that the League of Women Voters has joined in both the Washington State and Arkansas cases as an opponent of term limits. The reason the League should accept and support the term limits effort, rather than attack and denigrate it, is found in the League's own history. The vote for women was obtained by getting it state by state. A frontal assault on Congress for a national amendment would have failed until after 1916, when women had won full voting rights in 15 states. In short, the women who created the League gained their great success using exactly the same method of civic change that supporters of term limits are using today.

> ***The League of Women Voters Option***
> It is much more fun to sit on the sofa with the rich and powerful than to march in the streets for social justice. Even descendants of the struggle for the vote for women can be tempted to abandon principle for pleasure.

When the League attacks term limits today, it is attacking and betraying its own proud heritage.

The US District Court, in ruling on Speaker Foley's suit against the term limit initiative in Washington State, used two lines of reasoning to strike down the initiative for violating the US Constitution. The first was that it violated the First and Fourteenth Amendment rights of voters and candidates, respectively to freedom of political activity and equal protection of the laws. Little time need be spent on this line of reasoning, since identical arguments were made and rejected in *Legislature v. Eu,* the California decision upholding term limits left standing by the US Supreme Court.

These arguments will fail again — the counterargument is that the sovereign people have their own rights under the First Amendment to make their own judgment about the conditions under which candidates may run to represent them, in either state or federal offices.

The second line of reasoning that appeared in the Washington State case was also used in the Arkansas Supreme Court decision now before the US Supreme Court for review. That logic is that the Constitution, in Article I, Section 2, sets the "qualifications" for membership in Congress by age, citizenship and residency in the state (but not in the district) and that these qualifications cannot be added to or subtracted from, by law. For the House the qualifications are, attaining the "Age of twenty–five Years," having been "a Citizen of the United States [for] seven years" and being "an Inhabitant of [his] State."

This argument is based on a misreading of *Powell v. McCormack,* 395 US 486 (1969), in the US Supreme Court. This argument will be raised again in the present case, and needs to be examined.

Adam Clayton Powell was a flamboyant and corrupt congressman who regularly won reelection from his district in New York City. In 1967, the House decided it had had enough of Congressman Powell, and voted not to seat him when he arrived in Washington as the reelected member from New

York's 15th district. Powell then sued Speaker McCormack for a ruling that the House could not do that, and to regain his seat.

The House excluded Congressman Powell under Article I, Section 5, which says, "Each House shall be the Judge of the Elections, Returns, and Qualifications of its own Members...." The Supreme Court concluded that the House could, as it had done to others, expel Congressman Powell for corruption in violation of House rules of conduct. But, it could not refuse to seat him first, since he was of the proper age, citizenship and residency, and had been duly elected from his district.

This is all that the *Powell* case decided. It had absolutely nothing to do with state election law, and even noted that Powell came to Congress with his certificate of election from the secretary of state of New York, in hand.

The problem with *Powell* is its language. It is far broader than the facts required, and that broad language has been seized on by the Washington State and Arkansas courts to bar limits by state action, a question not presented in *Powell.*

The Supreme Court quoted Alexander Hamilton, writing in *The Federalist,* "The qualifications of the persons who may chose or be chosen... are defined and fixed in the Constitution, and are unalterable by the legislature." In context, Hamilton was talking about *congressional* power, not state power, a difference that may be decisive in *US Term Limits v. Thornton.*

There is another constitutional provision, which the *Powell* court noted did not apply when a single House was acting to exclude or expel a member. That provision, Article I, Section 4, says, "The Times, Places and Manner of holding elections for Senators and Representatives, shall be prescribed in each State by the Legislature thereof; but the Congress may at any time by Law make or alter such Regulations...."

Proponents of term limits are arguing that they are permissible under this precise language about "times, places and manner," as have been other provisions of state election laws like requirements that certain state officials must resign from their present positions to run for Congress. These have been upheld by the Supreme Court.

Another factor in the test case is the Tenth Amendment. That provides, "The powers not delegated to the United States by the Constitution, nor prohibited by it to the States, are reserved to the States respectively, or to the people." The power of this Amendment was gutshot in *Garcia v. San Antonio Transit,* 469 US 528 (1985), when the Supreme Court reversed prior cases and ruled that the Tenth Amendment posed no legal barrier protecting the states from federal encroachment, but only offered a political remedy. However, with term limits, the states *are* applying a political remedy to straighten out an unwilling and unresponsive Congress.

The last important factor in the test case is constitutional history. The 17th Amendment in 1913 made senators popularly elected, rather than chosen by the state legislatures. It earned the vigorous opposition of Congress. (The House passed the proposed amendment five times between 1898 and 1910. Each time it died in the Senate without even the courtesy of a hearing.) Many states had changed their own election laws to make senators elected; and two–thirds of the states demanded a new, limited Constitutional Convention to write this Amendment. Only then did the Senate relent and pass the Amendment.

Likewise, the 19th Amendment to give women the right to vote earned adamant opposition from Congress. Not until 15 states had changed their election laws to give the right to vote to women, did Congress relent and pass that Amendment.

Both these Amendments are important to the Supreme Court's consideration of the test case on term limits. The Arkansas court could not agree on its reasons for holding limits unconstitutional as applied to Congress. Three judges wrote that it violated the "qualifications" clause per *Powell.* Two judges decided that *Powell* did not apply to state laws, but that national "uniformity" was required in provisions concerning congressional elections, so states could not act independently.

The history of the 17th and 19th Amendments belies the uniformity argument. If uniformity was a requirement, women would still not have the right to vote, and senators would still be elected by state legislatures rather than by the people.

If the uniformity argument had been knocked out, then the Arkansas Supreme Court would have ruled *for* congressional term limits, rather than against them.

The strongest argument for term limits is found in the dissent by two judges in Arkansas. They determined that the qualification clause is only a minimum. They conclude, "Justice Holmes observed that government is an experiment. The people are the conductors of that endless experiment and have the right to tinker with it as they choose, free of unwarranted interference." In short, since the people have the sovereign power, it is their right to decide the conditions of representation of their own senators and representatives, regardless of whether others in other states agree with them, now or later.

This analysis leads to the conclusion that the US Supreme Court will reverse the Arkansas Supreme Court, and rule that state–based term limits on members of Congress are constitutional. That decision will probably be based on the First and Tenth Amendments, and the history of the adoption of the 17th and 19th Amendments. It should also conclude that the *Powell* case has no application to the present case.

The Supreme Court's decision in *US Term Limits v. Thornton* should come down early in 1995. If that decision is favorable, a national term limits amendment will be only years away. Should it rule against the popular votes on this issue, then different methods leading to the same end will be pursued over a longer course of time.

11

Throwing Them *All* Out?

How Will Term Limits Become Universal?

The war for term limits has reached a point where a second front must be opened up. As described, all but one of the states in which the citizen initiative can pass limits on Congress should be completed in 1994. The exception is Mississippi, where the petitioning is complete, but the vote will not occur until 1995. Victory there is highly expected.

Term limits will never become universal, applying to all the members of Congress, until more than a majority of both houses are committed to limits. This can happen by choice, as members run and are elected on pledges of supporting term limits. More commonly, it can happen by force, as additional states impose limits through their election codes.

Actually, the operative turning point is when a majority of the majority of both houses of Congress are from term–limited states, or who believe in term limits regardless of the status of their own state's laws. The first order of business when every new Congress meets after the election of a new House and one–third new senators, is to choose leaders and establish operating rules. Party caucuses, for many years now the Democrats, agree to support their own choices on the floor. Therefore, the leaders and procedures chosen by the Democrats become the choices of the House and Senate.

The critical decisions that will change the function of Congress forever will occur in the organizing caucuses after the majorities in them are subject to limits either by compulsion or personal choice. The majority will recognize that unless they abandon the seniority system, all leadership positions forever will go to the minority of members from states without limits. Naked self–interest will be sufficient incentive to solve that potential problem.

In the same session of Congress, perhaps the one starting in January 1996, the House and the Senate will also take up the question of proposing a universal term limits amendment for all members of Congress. The logic is identical to that causing the end of the seniority system.

The strategy of term limit supporters therefore is about to change. Initiatives will continue for limits at the local level, but the state–level focus will shift to the state legislatures. Lobbying legislatures to pass laws is a different process from that of conducting initiative campaigns, but the basis is still the same. Both the carrot and the stick will be used.

Legislators will be offered the support of the most powerful citizen movement in the United States today, if they sign and keep pledges to their constituents to introduce and vote for term limits for Congress. Legislators will be assured the wrath of the same movement if they oppose or vote against term limits. As with most citizen–based lobbying efforts, quiet persuasion in office meetings will be combined with public demonstrations to display massive public support. Term limit organizations state by state will raise the money for detailed and sophisticated polls on support for limits.

Because public support for limits transcends all demographic boundaries, it will be possible to measure the demographics of the voters for any state representative or senator, and tell him or her with precision the level of citizen support for limits in that particular district. Almost never will it be below 55 percent. Sometimes it will be as high as 80 percent.

At the same time, major continuing organizations in each state — farmers in one state, oil and gas workers in another — will be urged to join the support for term limits regardless of their positions in the past. Their own members will be polled to demonstrate to their leaders they are bucking their own members unless they get on board.

All of the normal techniques used by any "outsider" organization to obtain legislative results in any state, will be employed by term limit supporters.

The heat was turned up in 1994 in elections. It will stay turned up in 1995 and beyond in state capitols. The pot will continue to boil; it will just move to another burner.

It is always wise in politics to have an alternative plan. Term limit supporters have one. Every state has dozens of existing organizations that rightly feel their issues would fare better in the hands of the people than in the hands of the legislature. They may have little use for one another's specific politics. But they can agree on one subject: their state should have the right of initiative and referendum for citizens.

So far, this book has discussed only initiatives, which are an offensive weapon, to do what the legislature refuses to do. Referenda are the flip side of the coin. They are a defensive weapon by which citizens can petition to put on the ballot an action the legislature has already taken, and by majority vote strike it down. Usually, these two powers are placed in a state constitution as a pair. Although term limit supporters have little use for the referendum, if supporting that would gain the initiative power they will do so.

Initiative and referenda have almost the same extraordinary support among the public as term limits do. Two states provide examples of how joint effort by disparate citizen action groups can seek to force through a legislature the establishment of these rights.

Mississippi created its initiative power two years ago, the first state in decades to do that. In South Carolina, an organization called V.O.I.C.E. (Voters Organized to Initiate Citizen Empowerment) is lobbying for the initiative. V.O.I.C.E. includes both liberals like the ACLU and the Rainbow Coalition and conservatives like the S.C. Policy Council and the S.C. Taxpayers Association.

Obtaining the initiative in order to obtain term limits later is what pool players call a two–rail shot. If the final objective cannot be reached directly, it can be reached indirectly. All the same political techniques of subtle and not–so–subtle persuasion can be used to obtain the right of initiative as to obtain a term limits law itself.

And if the simple route fails, the more complex route may have a better chance due to the combined impact of the disparate groups representing essentially all the citizens of the state in one capacity or another.

Where legislative action on term limits is the goal, as mentioned, limits supporters can accept the Utah proviso that the laws will not go into effect until 25 states total have acted. Only two more states will trigger this provision, and there are at least three obvious targets for legislative action now: New Hampshire, New Jersey, and Texas.

The ultimate goal, of course, remains a national, constitutional amendment. Texas plus any other state would put the amendment in the catbird seat in Congress because Texas has 30 members in the US House. North Carolina, with its 12 representatives, plus almost any other state, would accomplish the same result.

Although under Article V of the Constitution the ultimate goal must be two–thirds of both the House and the Senate (to pass a proposed constitutional amendment), the interim goal of a majority in both houses will probably suffice.

As discussed before, once a majority in both Houses are term–limited, the seniority system in Congress will die a quick and, to the Foley Forces, a painful death. Rather than hand over all positions of power in Congress to the nonlimited minority, the majorities will end seniority as the normal way to choose leaders.

The new leaders chosen will agree with the new majorities, that term limits should be established for Congress. Especially in the House, the personal opinions of leadership are essential to the passage, or blockage, of any legislative action. Former Speaker Tom Foley may be reelected a couple more times from his Spokane district, but he will no longer be the *bête noire* of term limits. He will watch from the sidelines as his pet hate becomes part of the Constitution.

Ratification of the Congressional Term Limits Amendment as the 28th Amendment should pose no problem, provided Congress proposes a real amendment rather than a fig–leaf one. First, the people have already voted, strongly in favor, in many states. Second, state legislatures in others will already have been softened up in the lobbying campaigns to obtain state laws on the subject.

Third and most important, the same engine for civic achievement will start up. The public interest favors term limits, but so do the private interests of the state legislators. If they want promotion to Congress before they are too old to seek it, term limits are in their interests as well.

Essential to all the efforts directed at the state legislators will be the "Voters Contract" — asking them to sign commitments made public to their constituents, not only to work for state–based federal limits, but to vote to ratify a "3 and 2" amendment when Congress passes it, and to reject any lesser amendment that Congress might try to slide through. The "3 and 2 Plan" requires three terms only for representatives, two terms for senators. It will be pointed out again and again that in special elections to fill US House vacancies in 1994, in Kentucky and Oklahoma, the winners had signed the "Voters Contracts," the losers who were initially favored, had not.

In both these instances, the winners were Republicans and the losers Democrats. However, at all levels the term limits movement is multi–partisan. All candidates, without exception, are invited to sign the Voters Contract. All who do so will be equally recognized for their position. There will be instances where Democrats sign and Republicans don't. The pendulum will swing in the other direction.

In the 1994 elections for Congress, the Democratic Congressional Committees are threatening to cut off Party support for any Democrats who sign one of these contracts. The Republicans are not much better, since their leaders are all threatened by term limits and their Party has refused to take any stand on the issue. Either way, and with independent and third–party candidates thrown in, decisions to sign Voters Contracts will be individual to each candidate. Only a general pattern of victory for signers and defeat for nonsigners regardless of party will break the back of the opposing Democratic and Republican leadership.

It might seem strange to place on the table a description of future strategy for any political organization. But the movement for term limits is an intensely public one. There are no secrets about what it is doing or where it is going. The sooner that die–hard opponents like Speaker Foley realize that the game is over and they have lost, the sooner they will abandon ship for more peaceful and

> ***The Swamp Water Theory***
> Congress will swallow anything, if you give it two choices and the other one is worse.

lucrative pursuits, just as a quarter of the California legislature did in 1992.

In the legislative arena there are usually three choices: act for a proposal, act against a proposal, or do nothing. The third choice, to do nothing, has a strong advantage. If the congressman takes no vote, but postures with enough subtlety and skill, both supporters and opponents of the issue at hand may continue to consider him a friend and support him. But as soon as a vote is cast, either supporters or opponents will be dissatisfied to some extent.

For term limits, the opposing sides are the people and the long–termers in Congress. The do–nothing option is especially attractive in that situation. Congressmen fear taking a recorded vote on the subject of term limits as Count Dracula feared a garland of garlic. Still, if enough pressure with the ability to harm congressmen is brought to bear, Congress will act.

Term limits for Congress are fast approaching the point where Congress will be forced to act, or suffer worse consequences for failure to act. Exactly that had to be done to Congress to obtain the 17th and 19th Amendments. Exactly that will be done to Congress to obtain the 28th — the Congressional Term Limits Amendment.

For many of the same reasons that the US Supreme Court will approve term limits, Congress will be forced to approve them and send them out for ratification by the states. Then, representatives and senators will function under the same political rules as presidents and vice presidents. They will come into office knowing exactly how long they can have, maximum, to do what they came for. They will apply themselves more to their tasks, and less to the treadmill of lifetime reelection. That will be the legacy of term limits.

Technical Appendix

Abandon hope, all ye who enter here.

Dante, *The Inferno*

Most people have a strong distaste for large doses of statistics, history and law. Others revel in such information. This appendix contains supporting material for *Why Term Limits?* Those who want such information are welcome to proceed. But all who venture beyond this point are warned they do so at their peril.

Table A

Major Contributors Against Term Limits , 1900–92

(Note: this is only a partial list, but is representative.)

Sources: Public records in the states; press accounts of elections.

In Arkansas (1992)

Arkansas Democratic Party	$30,000
Arkansas Farm Bureau Federation	30,000
Arkansas Chamber of Commerce	15,000

In California (1990)

[Note: unlike the other entries, these are mostly industry–wide figures, compiled by the *Los Angeles Times,* and published Oct. 30, 1990. The newspaper also identified the specific legislative interest of each donor.]

California Teachers Assn.	$204,000
horse racing industry	136,500
tobacco industry	111,000
trial lawyers industry	103,700
alcohol industry	56,000
California Medical Assn., Coop. of Amer. Physicians	35,000
film industry	21,000
surety insurance companies	20,000
So. Calif. Edison Co. and San Diego Gas & Electric Co.	20,000
Irvine Co.	20,000
Alamo Rent–a–Car	10,000

In California (1992)

BankAmerica Corp.	$25,000
Pacific Telesis Group	25,000
Assoc. of Calif. School Admin.	5,000
Hewlett–Packard Co.	5,000

In Michigan (1992)

Ford Motor Company	$30,000
Southern California Edison	15,000
Kellogg Company	10,000
Pacific Telesis	10,000
Philip Morris, Inc.	10,000
USX Corporation	10,000
Michigan Research Associates	8,000
Coastal Corporation	5,000
AFSCME	5,000
General Dynamics	5,000
United Steelworkers of America	5,000

In Nebraska (1992)

CARE–PAC	$5,000
Peter D. Hart Research Services	5,000
Mary A, Harding	5,000
Nebraska State Education Assn.	5,000

In Washington State (1991)

Philip Morris USA	$25,000
Washington St. Labor Council	24,500
Kaiser Aluminum	16,695
Wash. Federation of St. Employees	12,535
Aerospace Machinists	10,000
Assoc. of Trial Lawyers of Amer.	10,000
Boeing Corp.	10,000
Burlington Northern	10,000
National Rifle Assoc.	10,000
PULSE—Wash. Education Assn.	9,000
United Sign Associates	7,587
Pacific Public Affairs	6,758
US West Communications	5,500
Akin, Gump, Hauer & Feld	5,000
Aluminum Co. of America	5,000
Anheuser–Busch Companies	5,000
Central States Management Corp.	5,000
Consolidated Rail Corp.	5,000
Cox Cable	5,000
CSX Corp.	5,000

In Washington State (1992)

E.J. Gallo Winery	$25,000
Kaiser Aluminum	12,000
Washington Water Power	10,000
HERE, Washington, DC	10,000
Olin Ordnance	5,000
McAndrews & Forbes Holdings	5,000
Burlington Northern	5,000
Washington Coastal States	5,000
Federal Express	5,000
RJR Nabisco	5,000

Table B

Total Turnover and "Voluntary Quits," House of Representatives, 1790–1992

"Voluntary Quits" includes deaths and expulsions, not a consequential number. Prior to 1900, odd– and even–year elections are combined in next higher even–number. Congressional Research Service Report, "Reelection Rates of House Incumbents: 1790–1988," David C. Huckabee, March 16, 1989. National Journal, Nov. 10, 1990. *Congressional Quarterly Weekly Report,* Nov. 7, 1992.

Year	% of "Volun. Quits"	% of Total Turnover	Year	% of "Volun. Quits"	% of Total Turnover
1790	36.9	41.5	1840	35.1	46.3
1792	30.8	30.8	1842	62.8	76
1794	35.2	37.1	1844	39.5	51.1
1796	34.9	39.6	1846	48	54.7
1798	34.9	38.7	1848	47	57.4
1800	43.4	46.2	1850	44	58.2
1802	30.2	34	1852	48.7	63.8
1804	21.8	31	1854	41.5	62
1806	30.3	31.7	1856	32.5	49.2
1808	32.4	36.6	1858	33.3	49.6
1810	36.6	40.9	1860	36.8	53.5
1812	32.2	41.3	1862	43.4	61.5
1814	37.9	45.6	1864	26.9	46.2
1816	57.3	63.7	1866	27.3	38.2
1818	39.3	44.8	1868	38.7	48.3
1820	37.1	47.9	1870	32.1	50.6
1822	31.7	38.2	1872	29.6	48.2
1824	30.5	38.5	1874	31.9	60.6
1826	28.6	36.2	1876	27.1	47.3
1828	29.6	43.7	1878	30.7	44.7
1830	31.9	39	1880	21.5	35.5
1832	36.6	49.3	1882	29.4	49.2
1834	21.7	41.2	1884	24	41.9
1836	38.2	49.4	1886	24.3	39.4
1838	34.3	50.4	1888	22.8	37.2

Year	% of "Volun. Quits"	% of Total Turnover	Year	% of "Volun. Quits"	% of Total Turnover
1890	21.5	45.9	1940	6.4	17
1892	20.5	37.4	1942	9.2	24.6
1894	24.2	49.4	1944	6.9	17.9
1896	19.3	41.2	1946	8.5	24.6
1898	15.4	30	1948	8.1	27.1
1900	15.1	24.9	1950	8.1	15.8
1902	16.8	28	1952	12	15.6
1904	12.4	21.5	1954	6.4	12.9
1906	13.2	24.6	1956	5.7	10.6
1908	9.5	20.7	1958	9	18.2
1910	13.6	32	1960	7.3	13.8
1912	21.6	35.6	1962	7.1	15.4
1914	14	31.3	1964	8.7	20.9
1916	8.1	19.3	1966	5.5	16.8
1918	10.6	24.4	1968	6	9
1920	11.5	27.8	1970	7.8	12.9
1922	11.7	30.1	1972	10.3	16.1
1924	7.8	17.9	1974	10.1	21.1
1926	6.9	13.6	1976	11.7	15.4
1928	7.1	16.3	1978	12.4	17.7
1930	6.4	19.5	1980	8.5	17
1932	9.9	37.7	1982	9.7	18.6
1934	10.8	25.3	1984	6	9.9
1936	10.8	21.8	1986	9.7	11.5
1938	7.6	26.9	1988	6	7.6
			1990	6.9	10.3
			1992	15.4	25.3

Table C

Average Tenure, House of Representatives, 1952–90

Sources: *Congressional Directory* through 1985; *Congressional Quarterly Weekly Reports,* Oct. 11, 1986, Nov. 8, 1986. Jan. 7, 1989, Nov. 10, 1990; *Almanac of American Politics 1990,* National Journal, 1989.

Year	Average Tenure	Percent Freshmen	Year	Average Tenure	Percent Freshmen
1952	9.6	18%	1972	11.4	16
1954	10.4	11	1974	10.8	20
1956	11.0	9	1976	9.2	15
1958	11.2	18	1978	10.0	18
1960	11.6	13	1980	9.8	17
1962	11.4	15	1982	9.2	18
1964	11.0	19	1984	9.4	9
1966	11.2	14	1986	11.2	11
1968	11.4	8	1988	11.6	8
1970	12.0	11	1990	12.4	10

George Will's book, *Restoration,* notes at p. 90, "[b]etween 1860 and 1920, the average length of House service doubled from two to four terms." As the preceding Table B shows, prior to 1860 almost half of all congressmen were freshmen, meaning an even lower average than two terms or four years.

As the following Table D shows, the rise in tenure has occurred primarily among the *leaders* of the House, not the rank and file. But given the power of the leaders over the operation of the House, that is the source of the problem.

Table D

Average Tenure,
House Leaders, 1900–94

(every entry is the beginning of a Congress, except 1994)

Sources: Office of the House Historian (for leaders and years); *Members of the House of Representatives Since 1789,* Congressional Quarterly Press, 1988 (for dates of election).

Year	Average	Speaker	Year	Average	Speaker
1900	13.6	18	1948	20.6	36
1902	15.6	28	1950	22.6	38
1904	17.2	30	1952	25.8	28
1906	19.2	32	1954	25	40
1908	19.25	34	1956	27	42
1910	14	18	1958	27	44
1912	14.6	20	1960	29.8	46
1914	14	22	1962	25.4	35
1916	16	24	1964	24.6	37
1918	18	26	1966	26.6	39
1920	17.6	28	1968	28.6	41
1922	17.2	30	1970	25.6	24
1924	15.2	18	1972	24.8	26
1926	17.2	20	1974	21.6	28
1928	17.6	22	1976	21.6	24
1930	17.6	28	1978	23.6	26
1932	17.4	28	1980	20.4	28
1934	15.4	26	1982	22.4	30
1936	16.6	20	1984	24.4	32
1938	16.6	22	1986	23.2	32
1940	16.4	28	1988	24	34
1942	17	30	1990	19.6	26
1944	19	32	1992	22	28
1946	19.8	22	1994	24	30

Table E

Predictions of House Races in 1994

Notes: Incumbents are in bold type. Only three incumbents are predicted for defeat, their winning challengers are marked *. Level of certainty of victory is indicated by 1, 2, or 3, with 3 being the highest. Two incumbents are rated as tossups. For the 18 open–seat races not called, main challengers likely to win in November in the general election are listed.

Alabama		
1	**Callahan,** R	3
2	**Everett,** R	3
3	**Browder,** D	2
4	**Bevill,** D	3
5	**Cramer,** D	3
6	**Bachus,** R	3
7	**Hilliard,** D	3
Alaska		
AL	**Young,** R	3
Arizona		
1	no call, this race	
2	**Pastor,** D	3
3	**Stump,** R	3
4	Shadegg, R	1
5	**Kolbe,** R	3
6	**English,** D	3
Arkansas		
1	**Lambert,** D	3
2	**Thornton,** D	3
3	**Hutchinson,** R	3
4	**Dickey,** R	2
California		
1	**Hamburg,** D	3
2	**Herger,** R	3
3	**Fazio,** D	3
California *continued*		
4	**Doolittle,** R	3
5	**Matsui,** D	3
6	**Woolsey,** D	3
7	**Miller,** D	3
8	**Pelosi,** D	3
9	**Dellums,** D	3
10	**Baker,** R	3
11	**Pombo,** R	3
12	**Lantos,** D	3
13	**Stark,** D	3
14	**Eshoo,** D	3
15	**Mineta,** D	3
16	Lofgren, D	1
17	**Farr,** D	3
18	**Condit,** D	3
19	**Lehman,** D	3
20	**Dooley,** D	3
21	**Thomas,** R	3
22	Seastrand, R	1
23	**Gallegly,** R	3
24	* Sybert, R	2
25	**McKeon,** R	3
26	**Berman,** D	3
27	**Moorhead,** R	3
28	**Dreier,** R	3
29	**Waxman,** D	3
30	**Becerra,** D	3
31	**Martinez,** D	3
32	**Dixon,** D	3

California *continued*

33	**Roybal–Allard,** D	3
34	**Torres,** D	3
35	**Waters,** D	3
36	**Harman,** D	3
37	**Tucker,** D	3
38	**Horn,** R	3
39	**Royce,** R	3
40	**Lewis,** R	3
41	**Kim,** R	3
42	**Brown,** D	3
43	**Calvert,** R	3
44	Bono, R	1
45	**Rohrabacher,** R	3
46	**Dornan,** R	3
47	**Cox,** R	3
48	**Packard,** R	3
49	**Schenk,** D	3
50	**Filner,** D	3
51	**Cunningham,** R	3
52	**Hunter,** R	3

Colorado

1	**Schroeder,** D	3
2	**Skaggs,** D	3
3	**McInnis,** R	3
4	**Allard,** R	3
5	**Hefley,** R	3
6	**Schaefer,** R	3

Connecticut

1	**Kennelly,** D	3
2	**Gejdenson,** D	3
3	**DeLauro,** D	3
4	**Shays,** R	3
5	**Franks,** R	3
6	**Johnson,** R	3

Delaware

AL	**Castle,** R	3

Florida

1	no call, this race	
2	**Peterson,** D	3
3	**Brown,** D	3
4	**Fowler,** R	3
5	**Thurman,** D	3
6	**Stearns,** R	3
7	**Mica,** R	3
8	**McCollum,** R	3
9	**Bilirakis,** R	3
10	**Young,** R	3
11	**Gibbons,** D	3
12	**Canady,** R	3
13	**Miller,** R	3
14	**Goss,** R	3
15	no call, this race	
16	Coogler, R	1
17	**Meek,** D	3
18	**Ros–Lehtinen,** R	3
19	**Johnston,** D	
	Tsakanikas, R	
20	**Deutsch,** D	3
21	**Diaz–Balart,** R	3
22	**Shaw,** R	3
23	**Hastings,** D	3

Georgia

1	**Kingston,** R	3
2	**Bishop,** D	3
3	**Collins,** R	1
4	**Linder,** R	3
5	**Lewis,** D	3
6	**Gingrich,** R	3
7	**Darden,** D	2
8	**Chambliss,** R	3
9	**Deal,** D	3
10	**Johnson,** D	3
11	**McKinney,** D	3

Hawaii

1	**Abercrombie,** D	3
2	**Mink,** D	3

Idaho

1	**LaRocco,** D	3
2	**Crapo,** R	3

Illinois

1	**Rush,** D	3
2	**Reynolds,** D	3
3	**Lipinski,** D	3
4	**Gutierrez,** D	3
5	**Rostenkowski,** D	3
6	**Hyde,** R	3
7	**Collins,** D	3
8	**Crane,** R	3
9	**Yates,** D	3
10	**Porter,** R	3
11	Giglio, D	
	Weller, R	
12	**Costello,** D	3
13	**Fawell,** R	3
14	**Hastert,** R	3
15	**Ewing,** R	3
16	**Manzullo,** R	3
17	**Evans,** D	3
18	LaHood, R	2
19	**Poshard,** D	3
20	**Durbin,** D	3

Indiana

1	**Visclosky,** D	3
2	Hogsett, D	
	McIntosh, R	
3	**Roemer,** D	3
4	**Long,** D	2
5	**Buyer,** R	3
6	**Burton,** R	3
7	**Myers,** R	1
8	**McCloskey,** D	3
9	**Hamilton,** D	3
10	**Jacobs,** D	3

Iowa

1	**Leach,** R	3
2	**Nussle,** R	3
3	**Lightfoot,** R	3
4	Ganske, R	
	Smith, D	
5	McGuire, D	1

Kansas

1	**Roberts,** R	3
2	Brownback, R	1
3	**Meyers,** R	3
4	**Glickman,** D	3

Kentucky

1	**Barlow,** D	3
2	**Lewis,** R	2
3	Stokes, R	1
4	**Bunning,** R	3
5	**Rogers,** R	3
6	**Baesler,** D	3

Louisiana

1	**Livingston,** R	3
2	**Jefferson,** D	3
3	**Tauzin,** D	3
4	**Fields,** D	3
5	**McCrery,** R	3
6	**Baker,** R	3
7	**Hayes,** D	3

Maine

1	Dutremble, D	2
2	Baldacci, D	1

Maryland

1	**Gilcrest,** R	3
2	Brewster, D	1
3	**Cardin,** D	3
4	**Wynn,** D	3
5	**Hoyer,** D	3
6	* Dillon, D	1
7	**Mfume,** D	3
8	**Morella,** R	3

Massachusetts

1	**Olver,** D	3
2	**Neal,** D	3
3	**Blute,** R	3
4	**Frank,** D	3
5	**Meehan,** D	3
6	**Torkildsen,** R	3
7	**Markey,** D	3
8	**Kennedy,** D	3
9	**Moakley,** D	3
10	**Studds,** D	3

Michigan

1	**Stupak,** D	3
2	**Hoekstra,** R	3
3	**Ehlers,** R	3
4	**Camp,** R	3
5	**Barcia,** D	3
6	**Upton,** R	3
7	**Smith,** R	3
8	Chrysler, R	2
9	**Kildee,** D	3
10	**Bonior,** D	3
11	**Knollenberg,** R	3
12	**Levin,** D	3
13	Schall, R	1
14	**Conyers,** D	3
15	**Collins,** D	3
16	**Dingell,** D	3

Minnesota

1	Gutknecht, R	2
2	**Minge,** DFL	3
3	**Ramstad,** R	3
4	**Vento,** D	3
5	**Sabo,** D	3
6	Luther, D	2
7	**Peterson,** DFL	3
8	**Oberstar,** DFL	3

Mississippi

1	Ford, D	2
2	**Thompson,** D	3
3	**Montgomery,** D	3
4	**Parker,** D	3
5	**Taylor,** D	3

Missouri

1	**Clay,** D	3
2	**Talent,** R	3
3	**Gephardt,** D	3
4	**Skelton,** D	3
5	McCarthy, D	
	Sildon, D	
6	**Danner,** D	3
7	**Hancock,** R	3
8	**Emerson,** R	3
9	**Volkmer,** D	2

Montana

AL	**Williams,** D	3

Nebraska

1	**Bereuter,** R	3
2	**Hoagland,** D	3
3	**Barrett,** R	3

Nevada

1	**Bilbray,** D	3
2	**Vucanovich,** R	3

New Hampshire

1	**Zeliff,** R	3
2	**Swett,** D	3

New Jersey

1	**Andrews,** D	3
2	no call, this race	
3	**Saxton,** R	3
4	**Smith,** R	3
5	**Roukema,** R	3
6	**Pallone,** D	3
7	**Franks,** R	3
8	**Klein,** D	3

New Jersey *continued*

9	**Torricelli,** D	3
10	**Payne,** D	3
11	**Gallo,** R	3
12	**Zimmer,** R	3
13	**Menendez,** D	3

New Mexico

1	**Schiff,** R	3
2	**Skeen,** R	3
3	**Richardson,** D	3

New York

1	**Hochbrueckner,** D	3
2	**Lazio,** R	3
3	**King,** R	3
4	**Levy,** R	3
5	**Ackerman,** D	3
6	**Flake,** D	3
7	**Manton,** D	3
8	**Nadler,** D	3
9	**Schumer,** D	3
10	**Towns,** D	3
11	**Owens,** D	3
12	**Velazquez,** D	3
13	**Molinari,** R	3
14	**Maloney,** D	3
15	**Rangel,** D	3
16	**Serrano,** D	3
17	**Engel,** D	3
18	**Lowey,** D	3
19	Lynn, D	2
20	**Gilman,** R	3
21	**McNulty,** D	3
22	**Solomon,** R	3
23	**Boehlert,** R	3
24	**McHugh,** R	3
25	**Walsh,** R	3
26	**Hinchey,** D	3
27	**Paxton,** R	3
28	**Slaughter,** D	3
29	**LaFalce,** D	3
30	**Quinn,** R	3
31	**Houghton,** R	3

North Carolina

1	**Clayton,** D	3
2	Funderbunk, R Moore, D	
3	**Lancaster,** D	3
4	**Price,** D	3
5	Burr, R Sands, D	
6	**Coble,** R	3
7	**Rose,** D	3
8	**Hefner,** D	3
9	Balmer, R	1
10	**Ballenger,** R	3
11	**Taylor,** R	3
12	**Watt,** D	3

North Dakota

AL	**Pomeroy,** D	3

Ohio

1	**Mann,** D	3
2	**Portman,** R	3
3	**Hall,** D	3
4	**Oxley,** R	3
5	**Gillmor,** R	3
6	**Strickland,** D	3
7	**Hobson,** R	3
8	**Boehner,** R	3
9	**Kaptur,** D	3
10	**Hoke,** R	3
11	**Stokes,** D	3
12	**Kasich,** R	3
13	**Brown,** D	3
14	**Sawyer,** D	3
15	**Pryce,** R	3
16	**Regula,** R	3
17	**Traficant,** D	3
18	no call, this race	
19	**Fingerhut,** D	2

Oklahoma

1	no call, this race	
2	**Synar,** D	3
3	**Brewster,** D	3
4	no call, this race	
5	**Istook,** R	3
6	Lucas, R	1

Oregon

1	**Furse,** D	3
2	Cooley, R Kupillas, D	
3	**Wyden,** D	3
4	**DeFazio,** D	3
5	Webber, D	1

Pennsylvania

1	**Foglietta,** D	3
2	Fattah, D	2
3	**Borski,** D	3
4	**Klink,** D	3
5	**Clinger,** R	3
6	**Holden,** D	3
7	**Weldon,** R	3
8	**Greenwood,** R	3
9	**Shuster,** R	3
10	**McDade,** R	3
11	**Kanjorski,** D	3
12	**Murtha,** D	3
13	**Marg.–Mezvinsky,** D	3
14	**Coyne,** D	3
15	**McHale,** D	3
16	**Walker,** R	3
17	**Gekas,** R	3
18	Doyle, D McCarty, R	
19	**Goodling,** R	3
20	Mascara, D	1
21	DiNicola, D McConnell, R	

Rhode Island

1	Kennedy, D	2
2	**Reed,** D	3

South Carolina

1	Harrell, R	2
2	**Spence,** R	3
3	no call, this race	
4	**Inglis,** R	3
5	**Spratt,** D	3
6	**Clyburn,** D	3

South Dakota

AL	**Johnson,** D	3

Tennessee

1	**Quillen,** R	3
2	**Duncan,** R	3
3	Wamp, R	1
4	Hilleary, R Hoover, D	
5	**Clement,** D	3
6	**Gordon,** D	3
7	Byrd, D	1
8	**Tanner,** D	3
9	**Ford,** D	3

Texas

1	**Chapman,** D	3
2	**Wilson,** D	3
3	**Johnson,** R	3
4	**Hall,** D	3
5	**Bryant,** D	3
6	**Barton,** R	3
7	**Archer,** R	3
8	**Fields,** R	3
9	**Brooks,** D	3
10	Doggett, D	2
11	**Edwards,** D	3
12	**Geren,** D	3
13	**Sarpalius,** D	3
14	**Laughlin,** D	3
15	**de la Garza,** D	3

Texas *continued*

16	**Coleman,** D	3
17	**Stenholm,** D	3
18	Lee, D	3
19	**Combest,** R	3
20	**Gonzalez,** D	3
21	**Smith,** R	3
22	**DeLay,** R	3
23	**Bonilla,** R	3
24	**Frost,** D	3
25	Bentsen, D Fonenot, R	
26	**Armey,** R	3
27	**Ortiz,** D	3
28	**Tejeda,** D	3
29	**Green,** D	3
30	**Johnson,** D	3

Utah

1	**Hansen,** R	3
2	**Shepherd,** D	3
3	**Orton,** D	3

Vermont

AL	**Sanders,** Indep.	3

Virginia

1	**Bateman,** R	3
2	**Pickett,** D	3
3	**Scott,** D	3
4	**Sisisky,** D	3
5	**Payne,** D	3
6	**Goodlatte,** R	3
7	**Bliley,** R	3
8	**Moran,** D	3
9	**Boucher,** D	3
10	**Wolf,** R	3
11	**Byrne,** D	3

Washington

1	**Cantwell,** D	3
2	Shin, D	1
3	* Moyer, R	2
4	**Inslee,** D	3
5	**Foley,** D	3
6	**Dicks,** D	3
7	**McDermott,** D	3
8	**Dunn,** R	3
9	**Kreidler,** D	3

West Virginia

1	**Mollohan,** D	3
2	**Wise,** D	3
3	**Rahall,** D	3

Wisconsin

1	**Barca,** D	3
2	**Klug,** R	3
3	**Gunderson,** R	3
4	**Kleczka,** D	3
5	**Barrett,** D	3
6	**Petri,** R	3
7	**Obey,** D	3
8	**Roth,** R	3
9	**Sensenbrenner,** R	3

Wyoming

AL	Chamberlain, R or, Cubin, R	

Per *Roll Call* newspaper on June 21, 1994, two incumbents were defeated in primaries, two died, and 49 have either resigned (2), retired (26), were defeated in bids for other offices (2), or are now running for other offices (19). The other offices being sought are governor (6) and senator (13).

Table F

Total Fundraising, House Candidates, 1976–92, District Size and Fundraising by Categories, 1985–92

Federal Election Commission Report, 4 March, 1993. Federal Election Commission Report, 5 May,1988.

Winners, Total Fundraising

	(millions)	average
75-76	$42.5	$97,700
77-78	60.0	137,900
79-80	86.0	197,700
81-82	123.1	283,000
83-84	144.8	332,900
85-86	172.7	397,000
87-88	191.0	439,100
89-90	198.3	455,900
91-92	232.9	535,400

Average House District Size

92	584,900
90	570,300
88	560,600
86	550,500
84	540,600
82	531,900
80	519,200
78	499,800
76	492,000

Incumbents, Fundraising, PAC & Individual Contributions

	average	PACs	Individ.
85-86	377,200	26.3%	67.6%
87-88	424,700	28.9%	66.2%
89-90	444,700	24.2%	67.6%
91-92	547,200	31.9%	65.7%

Challengers, Fundraising, PAC & Individual Contributions

	average	PACs	Individ.
85-86	65,000	18.6%	53.8%
87-88	73,000	22.6%	52.4%
89-90	68,000	15.7%	52.4%
91-92	81,000	13.9%	52.0%

Open–Seat, Fundraising, PAC & Individual Contributions

	average	PACs	Individ.
85-86	197,700	21.0%	51.4%
87-88	196,500	20.6%	47.2%
89-90	206,600	24.5%	47.9%
91-92	171,100	21.2%	51.8%

Table G

Public Approval of Congress, 1963–94

Year	% Approval	Year	% Approval
1963	35	1981	38
1964	64	1982	29
1965	71	1983	33
1966	54	1984	32
1967	41	1985	53
1970	32	1986	42
1971	26	1987	42
1974	47	1988	42
1975	29	1989	46
1976	24	1990	46
1977	34	1991	32
1978	29	1992	18
1979	20	1993	24
1980	25	1994	29

Sources: The Harris Poll for 1963–71, 1984–85, 1989, 1990; The Gallup Organization for all other years.

Note: the poll nearest to June 30 was used for each year; "in years not shown, neither one polled on this issue."

Table H

Public Opinion on Term Limits, 1947–93

All polls are from the Gallup Organization unless otherwise noted.

Poll Date	Favor	Oppose	Undecided
Feb. 1947	54	39	7 (for Senators)
Apr. 1952	63	24	13
(Question changed to, "Are limits a good idea," for this poll only.)			
Feb. 1955*	39	49	12 (for Senators)
Mar. 1961	51	34	15
Feb. 1964	49	38	13
Jan. 1969	45	45	10
Nov. 1977	60	30	10
Apr. 1981	61	32	7
Nov. 1990	67	30	3
Aug. 1992 [1]	69	24	7
Oct. 1993 [2]	76	20	4
Nov. 1993 [3]	80	17	3

* This was the last time that the public agreed with the consistent and overwhelming position of Congressmen, their staff, and lobbyists, that term limits for Congress are a bad idea.

1. *Time*/CNN Poll by Yankelovich Clancy Shulman.
2. *Wall Street Journal*/NBC News.
3. ABC News/*Washington Post.*

Table I

Opinion of Congressional Staff, Bureaucrats and Lobbyists on Term Limits, 1992

Source: Executive Interviews by the Gallup Organization, August and September, 1992, of 300 randomly–chosen opinion leaders — 100 career federal executives, 100 congressional aides, and 100 lobbyists.

"No opinion," "don't know," or "refused" answers averaged 2–3 percent. Those have been eliminated.

		Aides	Execs.	Lob'ists	Total
Are you "satisfied or dissatisfied with the way things are going in the US?"	Satisf. Dissatis.	24% 74	25% 72	9% 89	19% 78
Congress is "reasonably well serving the people"	Agree Disagr.	60 36	36 63	25 74	40 57
"Do you favor or oppose public funding of congressional campaigns?"	Favor Oppose	52 47	57 42	49 49	53 46
"Do you favor or oppose new limits on campaign contributions"	Favor Oppose	87 9	80 16	78 18	82 14
"Do you favor or oppose public funding of congressional campaigns?"	Favor Oppose	15 85	60 39	52 47	42 57
"Do you favor ending public funding for congressional mailings?"	Favor Oppose	25 73	50 46	36 59	37 59

Interestingly, when the sample was asked how long they had held *their* jobs, 64.3% said 5 years or less; only 35.3% said 6 or more years.

Table J

Current Term Limits Efforts
Status of Statewide Efforts, as of July 1, 1994

States	Status, Petitions	Type of Limit
Alaska	on target	federal
Colorado	on target	local, shortens federal
Dist. of Col.	on ballot	local
Idaho	on target	federal, state, local
Illinois	blocked in court	state
Maine	on target	federal
Massachusetts	on target	federal, state
Mississippi	on target, for '95	federal, state, local
Nebraska	on target	federal, state, local; replaces '92 initiative
Nevada	on target	federal, state, local; replaces '92 initiative
North Dakota	on target	state, county, federal
Oklahoma	on ballot, in court	federal
Utah	on target	federal, state, county

Status of Local Efforts, as of July 1, 1994;
Larger Cities Expected on Ballot, Fall 1994

Akron — Ohio
Baltimore — Maryland
Chattanooga, Nashville, Knoxville — Tennessee
Green Bay, Madison, Milwaukee — Wisconsin
Lawrence, Kansas City, Topeka — Kansas
Minneapolis — Minnesota
Spokane — Washington

If all larger cities vote yes, 18 of the 25 largest US cities will have some form of term limits as of November 8.

Now expected for 1995

Columbus — Ohio
Seattle — Washington
St. Paul — Minnesota

More than 100 local jurisdictions now have limits; that should more than double this fall.

Bibliography

Books

Benjamin, Gerald and Malbin, Michael, editors, *Limiting Legislative Terms,* Congressional Quarterly Press, Washington, D.C., 1992. Excellent statistics, schizophrenic since 11 authors wrote it; favors and opposes term limits.

Coyne, James and Fund, John, *Cleaning House: America's Campaign for Term Limits,* Regnery Gateway, Washington, D.C., 1992. Excellent anecdotal information about abuses within Congress and special privileges of members that favor reelection, limited coverage of strategy, tactics, and other aspects of current and pending term limits efforts; favors limits.

Felton, Eric, *The Ruling Class,* Heritage Foundation, Washington, D.C., 1993. Analyzes the legislative process, especially the power of special interests in legislation, staff work, and the reelection of incumbents; favors term limits.

Hamilton, Madison, Jay, *The Federalist,* 1788. This remains the best-written, most compelling text on American political theory. Every concerned citizen should have a copy, one indexed by subject and keyed to the Constitution; favors "rotation in office."

Jackley, John, *Hill Rat,* Regnery Gateway, Washington, D.C., 1992. Personal story of what is involved for the usually young and eager assistants who staff the Congressional offices; takes no position on term limits.

Jackson, Brooks, *Honest Graft,* Farragut Publishing, Washington, D.C., 1990. Gives names, dates and places on the flow of money from special interests to congressional leaders; no position on term limits.

Malbin, et al, editors, *Vital Statistics on Congress, 1991-1992.* No text or discussion, just statistical analysis of members of Congress and their elections; excellent reference work; takes no position on limits.

Meiners, Roger and Miller, Roger, *Gridlock in Government: How to Break the Stagnation of America,* Free Congress Foundation, Washington, D.C., 1992. Concerned mostly with Congressional operations and fundraising from special interests, explains why PAC contributions go to all incumbents, even those who apparently oppose the views of donors; favors limits.

O'Rourke, P.J., *A Parliament of Whores,* Atlantic Monthly Press, New York, 1991. Biting humor, close to the truth, takes no position on anything.

Payne, James, *The Culture of Spending,* ICS Press, San Francisco, Calif., 1991. Good analysis of institutional imperatives that compel long-term members of Congress to spend more and more money on programs favored by special interests; favors term limits.

Stern, Philip, *Still the Best Congress Money Can Buy,* Regnery Gateway, Washington, D.C., 1992. Excellent on the flow of money from PACs into incumbent reelections; no position on limits.

Will, George, *Restoration: Congress, Term Limits and the Recovery of Deliberative Democracy,* The Free Press, New York, 1992. Long on history and philosophy, short on statistics, results, and law of term limits effort; favors limits.

Articles

Alexander and Bhojwani, "Term Limits and Election Reform," presented at the Term Limit Conference, University of California, Irvine, May 31-June 1, 1991; opposes limits.

Armor, John, "More Light, Less Heat: Term Limitations and Ticket-Splitting in a Half Century of Gubernatorial Elections," presented at Annual Meeting of the Public Choice Society, New Orleans, March 21, 1991; favors limits.

Gorsuch, N., and Guzman, M., "Will the Gentlemen Please Yield? A Defense of the Constitutionality of State-Imposed Term Limitations," 20 Hofstra Law Review 341, 1991. Excellent discussion of Framers' views; favors limits.

Greenburg, Dan, "Term Limits: The Only Way to Clean Up Congress," Heritage Foundation Backgrounder No. 994, August 10, 1994. Good general discussion; favors limits.

Kobach, Kris W., "Rethinking Article V: Term Limits and the Seventeenth and Nineteenth Amendments," 103 *Yale Law Journal 7*, May, 1994, pps. 1971-2007; favors limits.

Leahy, Norman, "Why Big Business Hates Term Limits," US Term Limits Foundation *Outlook Series,* Vol. 2, No. 1, February, 1993; favors limits.

Petracca, Mark, "Predisposed to Oppose: Political Scientists and Term Limitations," *Polity,* 24, Summer, 1992, pps. 657-672; favors limits.

Court Decisions

United States cases:

Burdick v. Takushi, 112 S Ct 2059 (1992). Decided that a total ban on write-in votes by residents of Hawaii did not violate their First or Fourteenth Amendment rights, and were within the powers of the state over its own election laws under Article I, Section 2 of the US Constitution that gives states power over the "times, places and manner" of federal elections.

Powell v. McCormack, 395 US 486 (1969). Because this case was used by two lower courts and must be distinguished by the US Supreme Court, it is discussed in the text at page 123.

Arkansas

US Term Limits v. Hill, 316 872 SW2d 349 (1994), *cert. granted,* 62 USLW 3835 (June 20, 1994). In a split decision over a strong dissent, the Arkansas Supreme Court upheld limits on terms of state officials, but struck them down with respect to members of Congress. The 5- judge plurality could not agree on a reason for their conclusion. Three judges held that the initiative created an "additional qualification" to be elected to Congress, which was invalid under *Powell v. McCormack,* 395 US 486 (1969). Two judges thought *Powell* did not apply, but struck the initiative on grounds that federal constitutional change required "unanimity" across the country. Two judges dissented on the grounds that *Powell* did not apply, that unanimity was not required, and that the ultimate sovereignty rested with the voters and their will should be carried out. This is the test case in the US Supreme Court.

Oklahoma

In Re: Initiative Petition No. 360, State Question No. 662, Case 82,648, July 19, 1994. The Oklahoma Supreme Court ruled that Initiative 360, limiting the terms of members of Congress from that state, should go on the ballot, and that determination of its constitutionality would be made after the election, and after the US Supreme Court issued its decision in *US Term Limits v. Thornton.* On much the same reasoning as this case, every legal challenger to all term limit initiatives (there may be dozens of them) should be delayed until after the people get to vote on them.

Nevada

Stumpf v. Lau, 839 P2d 120 (1992). In a divided decision the Nevada Supreme Court ruled 3-2 that *Powell* applied, and Nevada voters could not restrict terms of their members of Congress. They also offered technical reasons for their decision to strike the initiative from the ballot prior to the election. The dissent, as in Arkansas, said that *Powell* did not apply. Term limit supporters in Nevada have cured the technical problems, repetitioned, and the issue should be on the ballot there in 1994.

Washington State

Thorsted v. Gregoire, 841 F Supp 1068, (W.D., Wash. 1994). The United States District Court for the Western District of Washington ruled on a suit by Speaker Tom Foley, four voters, and the League of Women Voters of Washington, that Initiative 573, just passed by the voters there, violated the US Constitution and struck it down. The Court relied primarily on the *Powell* case in concluding the initiative impermissibly added a "qualification" to be a member of Congress. The Court also concluded that First and Fourteenth Amendment rights of the plaintiffs had been violated. Those issues were addressed and disposed of in *Legislature v. Eu,* (see page 120). The *Powell* issue is now before the Supreme Court in the test case now pending. The *Thorsted* case itself has been appealed to the US Ninth Circuit Court of Appeals, where it has been briefed, argued, and is awaiting decision.

You Can Help Give Congress Back to the American People!

By giving copies of this term limits handbook to your friends, your local media outlets, your elected officials, and to local political activists, you can help create hundreds of thousands of volunteers for term limits initiatives all across America.

Only if tens of thousands of citizens like you bring the term limits idea to the grass roots can we defeat the lobbyists and special interests—and the millions of dollars of PAC money they use to influence Congress! ***Please order today!***

Special Bulk Copy Discount Schedule

1 book $9.95	25 books $85.00
5 books $29.00	50 books $145.00
10 books $39.00	100 books $275.00

All prices include both postage & handling.

. . . .

JAMESON BOOKS, INC.
P.O. BOX 738
Ottawa, IL 61350

ORDER TOLL-FREE
800-426-1357

Please send me ____________ copies of John Armor's *Why Term Limits?* so I can help your battle for term limits campaigns all across the USA!

Enclosed is my check for $______________ or please charge my ☐ Mastercard ☐ Visa

No. ________________________ Exp. Date __________

Signature ________________________________

Name ___________________________________

Address _________________________________

City ___________________ State _____ Zip __________

Illinois residents please add 6% sales tax. Please allow 2 weeks for delivery.